# PONCING AROUND

## the Stage in Tights

# PONCING AROUND

## the Stage in Tights

Published by Brolga Publishing Pty Ltd
ABN 46 063 962 443
PO Box 452
Torquay 3228 VIC
Australia

email: markzocchi@brolgapublishing.com.au


ISBN: 978 17636-80173

Printed in Australia
Cover design by Luke Harris, WorkingType Studio
Typeset by WorkingType Studio

Cover photos:
Front cover: The Lord High Cook, Act 2 The Gondoliers 1989.
Back cover: A Ghostly Ancestor Act 2 Ruddigore 1990.

*To David and Barbara*

*Thank you for opening the door to the world of musical theatre and inviting me in.*

# Contents

# Act One

*The Squeeze –Your-Cheeks Together Tenor*

OR

*Poncing Around The Stage In Tights.*

Memories and reminiscences of 33 years with the Latrobe Light Opera Society and its metamorphosis The Latrobe Theatre Company, which will be henceforth be known as the LLOS and LTC respectively.

From the outset this is definitely NOT a history of either of those entities, just my recollection of the many fun moments [and occasional not-so-fun moments]I saw and had with them. Other people may have seen or were involved in these occurrences and formed a completely different take on them. So be it. I will leave the writing of a definitive history to someone who wishes to undertake that task and probably has more talent when it comes to writing proper history. Please also bear in mind that, in the immortal words of the great Dame Anna Russel, "I'm not making this up, you know!"

I first encountered the LLOS when early in the year of Our Lord 1976 I went to the first practice session for their upcoming production of "The Merry Widow". The obvious question is how did things get to this? So before crossing the threshold let me turn back a few years. I believe this process is now known as filling in the back story.

# PROLOGUE

I came to Morwell in February 1975 as a newly minted dentist coming to work in my first job after being allowed to put important-looking letters after my name. At that time I reckoned I knew everything about dentistry and about 90% of everything else. It did not take long to learn that I knew bugger-all about either. Working in a country town will do that and I am still mighty grateful that it did.

Drs.Eves and Milner had a large and exceedingly busy practice which employed a number of dental nurses with whom I became friendly and also with some of their families. One such family were the Dalgleishes, Mac, Jan their two sons and their daughter Judy who had possibly drawn the short straw and hence was my nursing assistant. So how come I was interested in Light Opera instead of what might have been considered more manly pursuits? Please bear with me as we go back a few more years.

# When I was a Lad

I grew up in the suburb of Malvern and attended De La Salle College from grade 4 until Matriculation. My parents were devout Catholics but not fanatical. My father often called his cousins' families more Catholic than the Pope. Nevertheless religious observance was a daily feature of our family life. It so happened that our parish, St. Josephs, had a boy's choir which was held in high regard in choral circles in Melbourne. It later came to include adult male voices as well. Two of my brothers and I were auditioned for enrolling in the choir and we all were successful. My older brother left shortly after as his voice broke. My younger brother and I were taught to sing by a wonderful choirmaster and organist named Hans Janssen who had emigrated from the Netherlands. I was also a member of the school choirs, firstly as a first soprano until my voice broke and later as a first tenor in the senior schools' men's choir. Strange as it may seem, I can pinpoint the exact day my voice broke.

As the lead soprano I had a solo descant to sing in the Gloria of the High Mass for Easter Sunday 1962. I was 13 years old. And it was now of all times and places that Mother Nature showed herself to be the fickle bitch she is. As my angelic soprano voice was climbing to the ethereal heights suddenly there was NOTHING...As my voice was descending, [as also,I suppose, were my testicles]notes re- appeared. I can still see the horrified look on Harry Janssen's face. Having this happen in front of a packed church was mortifying, with the long term result of this being a lifelong case of severe stage fright. The choir itself was disbanded only a year or two later as the liturgical changes wrought by the Vatican Council made trained choristers redundant.

The historical Latin Sacred Music was jettisoned and replaced by any motley group of adenoidal schoolchildren accompanied by an atonal nun with a questionably tuned guitar singing an abomination called a Folk Mass. And the great pipe organ in the church was dismantled as it was no longer required. Such vandalism had not been seen in a Catholic Church since the Reformation. Sic Gloria mundi transit.

On entering University in 1968, singing in choirs was the last thing on my mind. It was 1968. I was 18. Flower power was the fashion of the day and “Make Love not War” the mantra. The place was surrounded by pubs and full of hot and cold running women. Choral singing? Study? Bugger that! Apart from study, of which I did very little in my first year and subsequently had to repeat, my musical interests were rock and roll and funnily, Irish folk music and Australian bush music which was big at that time .That might have been the result of having a large dose of Irish ancestry. Instead of looking after the voice I gave it a real hard time. Monumental piss ups with the Fenian Society and the Folk Music Club did it no great service, nor did the riotous Friday nights singing [?] with the Bushwhackers and Cobbers at The Polaris Inn in Carlton. Of course, pursuit of the feminine sex and consumption of alcohol were integral parts of that environment.

It was the former that brought me into the world of musical theatre and G&S in particular. I had become friends with some girls who were student teachers and their teaching college was putting on a production of “Iolanthe” and men were needed for the chorus of peers. Yours truly saw an opportunity to press his suit with a lass he had his eye on, so was easily inveigled into auditioning. He was also keen to press quite a number of other things given half a chance. Being inveigled by the object of one’s desires is quite painless, even pleasurable. As the remaining fragments of the voice could still hold a tune I was in and to some amazement as a 1$^{st}$ Tenor. The show was a success but the lass who had inveigled me, got seriously inveigled with another member of the peers chorus. Bastard! However my lust, although unrequited, did enable me to overcome my stage fright and the other result was that I loved being in the show especially at the end, because the sound of an audience applauding you is a feeling like no other. The after show party wasn't too bad either. A chance for more suit pressing, only this time at a different dry cleaners'. This was also my first experience of poncing around in white tights.

# Act One

So here we are about to audition for a return to the stage. Except that there was no audition, at least, not for the chorus. I have no idea whether there were auditions for principal roles as I had no knowledge of that parallel universe. So whoever turned up and was upright and more or less mobile enough to get on and off the stage without outside assistance, and could afford the membership fee as well as the cost of the book, was in. All this was to take place in the" Hut". Before we enter the Hut, it needs a brief description. The LLOS was the proud tenant of the rear half of a large Nissan hut in Driffield Rd., at the bottom end of Morwell. It was where costumes were stored and sets constructed, although sets in those days were usually about four painted flats and a backdrop. It was also where rehearsals took place. It had power, lights, lockable doors and toilets, all of which were appreciated. What it did not have was insulation or any heating or ventilation other than leaving the doors open. As you might have guessed, it was brutally hot in summer and bitterly cold in winter. Sitting through rehearsals in July and August took some stamina. It also had a jerry built mezzanine floor for the storage of costumes in a large plastic wardrobe to keep dust at bay. Unfortunately it was not quite so successful at keeping the mice at bay. It was accessed by an equally rickety set of steps. Modern OH&S would have conniptions.

Little did I know that on crossing the threshold into that first gathering I was joining an organisation that was to become an integral part of my life and some years later I was to become an integral part of its. And again, why was I doing this? I think it was to meet people outside my work environment, make some friends but also hoping to strike up a relationship with a member of the opposite sex. I was probably not fussy at the time whether such an outcome was to be temporary or permanent.

I was now to meet the first of a long parade of immensely talented and capable people that I have encountered in my 45 years of association with LLOS and LTC. That some people will feature more prominently in these reminiscences than others is not a reflection on the magnitude of their contributions but more on what I recall of them. The first of them I shall call the big 4.

The first is one person who stands out over all others: Barbara Derham.

Barbara was tall and had PRESENCE. When she entered a room all attention fell on her. She was an outstanding teacher of music who believed that every person had the capability to sing and to sing well and judging from what she got out of the raw material presented to her over the years, she was probably right. Barbara had a way of making you believe in yourself. She also had an eye and ear for people with talent and she would make extraordinary efforts to nurture that talent. Having gotten to know her over the later years I found her to be great conversation with a puckish sense of humour and a weakness for risqué [but not crude or outright blue] jokes. However, such humour had to have some wit about it. When she laughed her eyes truly sparkled. In what I would regard as the LLOS's golden era she was one of the main driving forces because she believed that just because we were an amateur company we did not need to be amateurish in what we did. Perfection was to be striven for and sometimes I think we bloody near achieved it.

Ruth Widdowson was Barbara's right hand person [?].Ruth was the rehearsal pianist and when the show actually got onto stage the lynch pin of the orchestra. Ruth would be there every rehearsal playing bits and pieces over and over again until we got it into our heads. She had the patience of Job and then some. She never lost her cool or got flustered. When something went awry musically during a show, it was through her that Barbara got things back on the rails.

She was also a damned good pianist and she had a very dry sense of humour. I used to call her "ginge" because of the colour of her hair and she would chide me for being cheeky. That sounds rather twee but so what. She was great fun. After watching rehearsals for all these years I believe there is a special place in heaven for rehearsal pianists. On their demise, they go straight there, as they have already served their time in purgatory.

And now may I present....David Pickburn.

David was another person of great talent and great humility. He was the son of an Anglican vicar who adored G&S. From his earliest years, G&S were part of his life. He knew every G&S intimately and could sing any male role in that repertoire although the lead tenor roles had him stretching a bit. He was a natural for the patter song parts in the G&S canon. He was another person who lit up a room on entry and could move from person to person with the studied ease of the school principal he would become. He would have been a great diplomat. However, his talent consisted of much more than just being a top performer on the stage. He was also a director and mentor. He would later go on to found youth theatre companies in order to foster talented youngsters. His encouragement of novices like me was invaluable. David was a member of the Apex club of Traralgon which was a Service Club [remember them?] for young men. I had just joined its counterpart in Morwell. Be assured, there was nothing secretive or sinister about Apex. The relevance of the Apex connection will become apparent in due course. So one of the things we had in common was a delight in having fun and David made sure he had his share. He was also a hard worker in getting his part in any production right. However, there were a number of times that patter songs got a bit jumbled or some dialogue inadvertently omitted which caused some scenes to be severely truncated. David would just sail through it with his usual nonchalance with the audience none the wiser about what had just happened. David also believed that excellence was to be the goal of every aspect of our productions. He was a lovely man to know.

And now, last but not in any way least, let's hear it for ....Jenny Johnston.

Where to start?? Jenny could do everything. She had a lovely lyric soprano voice and she could act. There was nothing wooden about her performances. She excelled at playing matriarchs, countesses, senior fairies etc. She really had stage presence and a wealth of stagecraft. But that was just one aspect of her talents. Jenny designed posters that would have impressed Toulouse-Lautrec. She designed AND painted whole stage sets and to top it off was an excellent milliner and she achieved all of this with only one hand. She would draw caricatures of members of the company that were brilliantly funny without being hurtful. Jenny also had an almost wicked sense of humour and a weakness for fart jokes. She also had a great talent to be able to re write the words of various G&S songs to make them relevant to local circumstances and were always very funny. She was also great fun to be with.

Her commitment to pursuit of excellence matched Barbara and David's.

With people like the above in charge this company could really go places. And it did!

All of the above were actively supported by their husbands and wives.[In those days partners were people you did business with.].The LLOS owed much to George Derham, Dr.Robin Widdowson, Jan Pickburn and Barry Johnston, three of whom became very much involved in the company in their own right.

Meanwhile, back at the Hut, the cast has assembled for the first skirmish. Principals and chorus, and the chorus,in size and variety, resembled something akin to what Moses would have shepherded across Sinai but minus the sheep and the goats. I think they had been separated.

We take our seats. We greet one another. The Principals are introduced and greeted with slightly thunderous applause. The Committee is introduced to polite applause. This is my first inkling that such an august body exists. Still, who cares about them? We were here to sing.

The momentous occasion arrives when all together we open our books to begin our assault on "The Merry Widow", music by Franz Lehar, English libretto by Phil Park. I am sorry that now I am going to inflict a case of "actus interruptus" just as we were about to get underway, as at this point some words about Mr.Park and his librettos need mentioning. Our friend Phil seemed to have cornered the market in the translation of European operettas from the original German into English. Now as everyone knows, the Germans were not renowned for their sense of humour. Don't forget they did start two world wars just for fun. So whatever nuggets of humour may have been in the original German, they had well and truly been eliminated in the translation. And a good deal of the other dialogue was as corny as the meadows in Oklahoma and as stilted as a marionette show. I present the following as evidence. I am not sure what show this came from but here it is....A character called Otto comes onto the stage looking for someone else, quite possibly the leading lady who, understandably, is trying to avoid him. This scenario may well have been played out off stage as well. He asks a third person where she might be and this is the reply."She's in the grotto, Otto" Any librettist who expects some poor schmuck of an actor to say that is really in a class of his own. Further encounters with Phil and his librettos in later productions only confirmed my opinion.

The Merry Widow is all about the goings on primarily in the Paris embassy of some bumpkin Eastern European kingdom.

Having now opened our books, Barbara introduces our first number. It comes from somewhere in the middle of the show where a party is being held at said embassy. Upstairs all the knobs are pissing it up on champagne whilst down in the back yard a crowd of ex pat bumpkins are getting stuck into their slivovitz or some other slavonic lunatic soup and want to start a wild dance. So we now begin to learn the song. It's called 'Mi Velimo Danse", translated as " I Want to Dance". Who would have guessed! What language that was I knew not. It could have been pidgin Esperanto for all I knew or cared as we were now learning our song to be sung in four parts. It's a good lively tune and just as we were really getting into it, it ends. After about three bloody minutes! When the show got to production that must have annoyed the stage crew no end as having got all the sets and chorus onto the stage, they then had to get them all off again three minutes later.

As time progressed we learned our parts and got to see the Principals strut their stuff. We also got to observe some of their peculiarities. The leading man had a beautiful tenor voice but the charisma of a corned beef sandwich. Consequently the romantic scenes did lack a bit of sparkle. This may also have been the result of his habit of arriving in the nick of time for his rehearsal still finishing his dinner which, more often than not, was pizza. I know this whole thing is set in Europe but I'm sure Lehar did not have pizza in mind when he wrote it. I can fully understand the leading lady being in a less than romantic mood when being serenaded with overtones of pepperoni. His use of some anti-dandruff shampoo might also have been helpful.

Rehearsal was now chuntering along, gaining momentum as we learned our music and the chosen few who were called upon to actually dance in the appropriate fashion at the appropriate time, mastered their task. Fortunately I was able to avoid that fate. Choreography and I were never comfortable together.

Friendships were made and enjoyment had and I was making gentle progress in a relationship with a beautifully structured young maid in the chorus. After all, I was a young man with a full head of hair and beard who, unlike the balding, fat–arsed, arthritic old wreck writing this memoir, cut quite a figure in flares and body shirts and, importantly, drove a new Toyota Celica! Really, who could resist?

As we all got to know each other it became customary that should someone have a birthday on a rehearsal night, a cake was produced and Happy Birthday sung in what sounded like 35 part disharmony. But we meant well.

Such a fate befell the object of my ardour. We all sang the song and someone amongst the ladies called "Happy 16$^{th}$ Birthday" WHAT??? I have been squiring a fifteen year old schoolgirl!!!And I'm 26.! She may have been 16 chronologically but anatomically she was some years older than that. Well, that certainly put the brakes on things {on both me and the Celica}.As much as I might have wanted to, getting tangled up in any way you may imagine with a 16 yr old schoolgirl would not have been a good career move. Thank God I had kept the sword in its scabbard which was now well and truly bolted and sealed shut. Damn and Blast. Thwarted again!

Time passed and show time approached and as it did I was becoming aware that I was in a Band of Brothers called the Mens' Chorus, henceforth to be known as the MC. Its counterpart on the other side of the gender divide we shall call the Female Chorus or FC. The pedantic amongst you may have noticed I did not use the term Womens Chorus and this is because I doubt that the ladies would have liked to have been described as the WC. During their idle moments the MC had a habit of re- writing the lyrics of the songs, usually in a smutty fashion.

And this brings us to another part of this much loved work. This occurs at a place called Maxims which is portrayed as a high class restaurant with entertainment provided by the Grisettes who would dance the CanCan. In reality it's a high class knock shop and the Grisettes are the in-house hookers. This is where the louche members of the embassy came for relaxation and perhaps some horizontal folk dancing. One of them sings of " how he always feels much better for meeting a Grisette". The MC thought "meeting" was not quite the word to describe what really would happen there, so another word was thought to be more accurate. Cryptic crossword clue...present participle attached to a cormorant. Very early in rehearsal some wit in the MC made a remark about grisly Grisettes. It soon became very obvious that there was absolutely nothing grisly about our Grisettes,mate! The LLOS/LTC would not feature a line up like that until the KitKat girls thirty years later in "Cabaret", with the singular exception of the three female leads in "Charlie Girl". This will become relevant to our final performance of the season.

It was also at this time we got to meet a whole host of people without whose efforts no show can happen. They were the set builders/painters, costumiers, make-up artists, stage crew and orchestra, lighting operators, ushers and more. I had no idea so many people were there just so I could ponce around in tights, which did happen when we dressed as peasants in kneebritches in our Mi Velimo moments.

Then it came to pass that Opening Night was upon us. I have a vivid memory of us all being on stage behind the curtains which would fly open as we launched into the opening number. My stage fright was in full flush. As the overture was being played I was as nervous as a dog shitting razor blades. Fortunately I was standing next to David Pickburn, aka Baron Zeta the Ambassador whose advice was to take a deep breath, look beyond the audience, squeeze your bum cheeks together and give it your all. It worked. Strange to say I cannot recall which venue hosted Opening Night, Traralgon Little Theatre or Morwell Tech School Hall.

In those days choreography was the province of principals as they could use the whole stage when it was bereft of the chorus. When the chorus was on stage there was not enough room to do much artistic movement. Choreography for the chorus consisted mostly of getting the mob onto the stage and off again within a respectable time frame without bumping the sets over. It did actually require some skill to achieve this.

The season rolled on and we all got into the swing of things and as I became more at ease I was able to notice things in the audience and in the venue generally. The first of these was the gathering of musicians at our feet that formed the orchestra. Our good fortune did not extend to a full orchestra .We made do with what was available. I remember us having the inimitable Ruth Widdowson on the piano, Kath Teychenne on violin and a couple of the local medicos, one who had a clarinet and another who had a bassoon. There were others but they have not stuck in the memory. Brass players seem to have got a gig if they could play more notes than raspberries in any given tune.

The season was approaching its end. Coming to a climax would be overstating the case. I cannot recall when we learned that it was customary for the LLOS to do its final show at a third and very different venue. No need to sell tickets for this one and no need for ushers and front of house as the venue was the Morwell River Prison Farm up in the hills behind the bustling town of Boolarra, nearly an hours' drive away.

For this one- off performance sets were reduced to a minimum. I thought that they already had been. The numbers in the chorus were cut dramatically. No one under 18 was permitted. Many in the FC and some in the MC were quite happy to forego the delights awaiting them. The numbers had to be reduced as the performance was taking place in the prisoners mess room and the stage was about the size of three billiards tables. The orchestra was also reduced to Ruth and a couple of others. To this day, I still don't know why we did this .A sense of Community Service? A masochistic desire to play in the worst venue possible? Whatever, we were up for the challenge!

The show opened to a subdued reaction but the audience did warm up, as evidenced by the whistles and laughs along with the occasional piece of advice that emanated from amongst them. And then the Grisettes made their entrance.

Well, pandemonium broke loose! I'm not sure that the prison authorities knew that a line of very attractive young women would be dancing a CanCan in a male prison as part of this cultural exercise. Needless to say the Grisettes were the hit of the night. Whoever came on after them was facing a lost cause.

After what seemed twenty encores the girls cried " Enough!!"and the show sputtered to its almost post-coital conclusion. When it came to taking their bows the Principals were greeted with polite applause, the chorus mild acknowledgement but when the Grisettes come on for theirs, further uproar. The beast within the inmates had been roused one more time. .For a moment it seemed like the warders might need to cool the boys down with the fire hose. Eventually everything settled down and the boys were escorted, whimpering, back to their cells.

We retired to sandwiches and tea with the governor and staff and then packed our things and buggered off home. What a night! I would not have missed it for the world. And I do not doubt that, with apologies to Dominic Behan, and The Dubliners, the old triangle certainly went jingle-jangle all along the banks, perhaps not those of the Royal Canal, but definitely those of the Morwell River. Those girls had made many a man happy that night.

How did I feel about being part of this Company? I had loved it and wanted more. Plenty more. What are we doing next? When are we doing it? Where are doing it?

Some time before the end of the season, the announcement was made that next years' show was to be my old friend, "Iolanthe". Whooppee!! I knew this one. White tights again! This was to be staged in July of 1977.

One thing I had learned was that I was amongst people who had talent by the bucketful; I had it by the teaspoonful. Yet somehow over the next thirty years I was able to parley it into 23 more shows. Be reassured dear reader, I will not be treating all of them in the same detail as this, although they all had their moments.

Unknown to me {only because in those days I never paid any attention to such things} a decision had been made by the Committee that brought about the first unpleasantness. It was decided that numbers had to be reduced to those who could actually sing and move in a fashion that corresponded with the rhythm of the music. If they could actually dance, then that was a bonus. Hence all prospective participants would have to audition and those accepted would need to be adults unless there were specific parts written for children. Much disgruntlement was expressed by those who brought their whole families along to be on the stage. It was unfortunate for those who could not pass an audition but if the Company was to raise its standard of performance, it had to happen, and it had to happen in all aspects of production, but a start was made with the performers themselves. An unfortunate result was that many of those in FC and to a lesser extent the MC, left, and were not seen again. One who was, was named Harry Dougan. Harry had been one the founding members of the LLOS.I did not know that and when this big headed know-all started giving him advice on stagecraft, all he did was give a wee smile {he was after all, Scottish} and say thank you. It took a while before I realised I had been gently given a slice of humble pie. What a gentleman!

Meanwhile I couldn't wait for the next show but I did have a small problem. I still was in contact with my young lady friend who we met earlier although our relationship was, by necessity, utterly Platonic. I may have raised the drawbridge but the castle was still being gently assaulted. What to do? Fate provided the answer when we were in rehearsal for Iolanthe. Auditions had been held and having passed same, we were off and running. I might add here that the audition was not terribly difficult. I also suspect that the WUBWT factor had come into play.{Warm, Upright, Breathing, With Testicles}. Testicles, my downfall once, now my saviour!

The Principal Cast was quite a line up. I may be wrong but I think Don Sykes who had a beautiful tenor voice and could act was Strephon, Jenny Johnston, Iolanthe, Val Wilson, the Fairy Queen, George Murphy, Mountararat, David Pickburn The Chancellor, Max Alvin, Private Willis, I don't recall who was Tolloler or who the lead soprano was. The pursuit of perfection was underway.

Then disaster struck. Val Wilson had a fall and broke her ankle and then George Murphy had a heart attack. Fortunately they recovered. With two principals out of action, the production time line, already tight, was hopelessly compromised .The decision was made to postpone the show until November.

So how did this help me out of my romantic dilemma? By giving me the opportunity to do what any man caught in my position would do; Run away! Run away! Far, far away!

I had decided over the Xmas break that, as I had no real ties to keep me here, I might head to the UK for a year or two on an extended working holiday, departing after the Iolanthe season had finished. Now that the staging of the show was not going to happen in July,

I had the opportunity to bring forward my departure date to late April. So I did.

My notice was given, travel arrangements made, bags were packed, lots of farewell drinks had and off I went. I hoped I hadn't broken a heart with my cowardice but what other options did I have?

# END OF ACT ONE

Post script to Act One. About twenty years later I unexpectedly met up with her again and we had coffee together and discussed how our lives had panned out. In the meantime she had married, had two kids, got divorced and was now about to get married again. She carried no animosity towards me at all, in fact I was forgotten fairly smartly as she soon met another bloke who she subsequently married. I'm still bigheaded enough to think that even if I didn't break her heart, I might have caused a temporary wee crack in it. And after talking about all that had happened over the years, we rose and went our separate ways. As she walked away, I could not help but notice she was still beautifully structured.

I've not seen her since.

INTERVAL

# ACT TWO, THREE AND FOUR AND A BIT

However, as my second northern hemisphere winter loomed on the horizon, I decided to come back home. Winter in the Latrobe Valley could be miserable enough but it paled into insignificance compared to the UK and even more so when the social conditions in the UK in the late seventies were so fraught. Another factor was that working for the NHS, it was hard to make any financial headway without cutting corners with your work as living costs were brutal, and so your standards were in danger of slipping unacceptably. From the day I graduated until the day I retired, I always prided myself on doing quality work. The importance of that had also been drummed into me by the aforementioned Drs.Eves and Milner. I was quite chuffed that when they decided to sell their Morwell practice they gave me the first option to purchase it. As I was still in London at this time, as well as having no experience in running a dental practice or, I might add, the required amount needed for purchase, I declined. But Morwell was at that time a booming, busy town so I decided to return there and set up a solo practice of my own. Another consequence of being in the UK was the lack of opportunity to go outside for months on end whilst spending far too much time in the pub, as the flat I shared with two other fellows had heating only in the miniscule lounge room. In winter, icicles formed around the INSIDE of the window frames because the draughts. It was warm and hospitable in the "Cherry Orchard". It was here that I developed a taste of English Real Ale. God bless you all at the Cherry Orchard. The practice premises itself was tiny and cramped with nowhere to sit and have lunch so we ate at the nearest cafe, which was an Italian restaurant. You can imagine what a regime of pasta most days, lots of ale and sod all exercise did for the waistline.

So at the end of November 1978, a rather hairier and bloated version of the svelte young thespian who had departed 18 months ago, returned. I was too late to see the LLOS production of Oklahoma!, but was told it was a success, as was the eventual season of Iolanthe the year before.

At this time I was busy setting up my practice and working long hours to build up the patient base so I initially declined to be in the productions for that year. I was also on a strict diet and exercise regime to counter the excess baggage I had brought back with me from the UK and it was working I'm glad to record. However the lure of the stage overcame my better judgement and I succumbed to the flattery that as a tenor I was really needed and Trial by Jury is only a short show. To me, at this time in my life, the word ego was definitely not a dirty word. I was not told that the rest of the program was to be excerpts { some unkind person might say rehashes} from Iolanthe, Merry Widow and Oklahoma!. Iolanthe and white tights again! As regards Oklahoma the only things I knew about it were that the corn was high as an elephant's eye and that poor Judd was dead. Possibly trod on by an elephant. Apart from that I have no recollection at all of that production. I did learn a lesson that I really was too busy to be involved in the production of "The Pirates of Penzance", scheduled for later in the year. What I had noticed was that only one venue was being used, the Traralgon Little Theatre. No more Morwell Tech School hall and no trips up the river to the prison. I may be wrong, but I suspect that the pandemonium caused by the Grisettes there had still not settled. At this point it is time to take another diversion and discuss the venues we had at our disposal.

In the 1970s the State Government had taken an active interest in both the visual and performing arts and a proposal that a new performing arts venue be provided in one of the major towns in Gippsland. Given its' population and economic clout to me the Latrobe Valley was the obvious choice, either Morwell or Traralgon.

This statement shows how naive I was. The idea that either of these would get such an asset without the other screaming blue bloody murder was wishful thinking in the extreme. So neither got it due to the intense, entrenched, and puerile rivalry between the two towns. The likely candidates were to be Warragul, the Latrobe Valley or Sale which was the service town for the gas and oil industry in Bass Strait. Unfortunately other factors came into play. Warragul was in the seat of Narracan, held by a senior government minister. Sale was also in a seat held by a member of the government but not of ministerial rank. The seat of Morwell, which incorporated Morwell and Traralgon, was held by the Opposition. You don't need to be genius to work out where that arts centre ended up and Warragul has enjoyed having that facility ever since.

In the early 1960s the Traralgon City Council had the foresight to include a proper small theatre along with the erection of a new town hall. At the time this was quite revolutionary. All the same it was built to a budget and many things that you would expect to be in any normal theatre were not there in this one. Both Morwell and Yallourn had town halls which were supposed to cater for such theatrical performances that local troupes may put on. In those days and well into recent times very few council members had the wit or even the desire to know that to stage a musical "play" as all too many of them deemed it, certain basic facilities were necessary. A notable exception to this was Lorraine Bartling, a councillor from both the City of Traralgon and later the Latrobe City, who was one of the very few who did. Their attitude was 'You've got a hall with a stage, what more do you want?" Plenty actually, but if you started to then tell them that, you could see ears close and eyes glaze over. If you were a football club, well, that was a very different matter.

What it did have was a cambered stage, curtains, reasonable acoustics, a reasonable bank of stage lighting, including a spot and a biobox from which a show could be run. It also had dressing rooms and a room that could be used as a green room. It had a proper box office as well and something which was quite revolutionary for its time, wheelchair access. It also had removable seating so that an orchestra "pit" could be created. When it came to the seating for the audience though, that was something else. The money to build the place must have run out before the seating was installed. Instead of the usual soft padded seats than could fold up, these were bright orange moulded plastic. More like a bucket than any theatre seat I have ever seen. It was many years before they were grudgingly replaced and lastly, it really was a LITTLE theatre. Once seats were removed to accommodate the orchestra the capacity of the place was 178 people. This meant we had to do many more performances to recoup our costs and hopefully a profit. One upside of having such an extended season was the opportunity for closer camaraderie to form in the MC. This was to have a significant and beneficial effect on the company's performances.

What it did not have were, in no special order of importance, a fly tower, orchestra pit, wings, and amazingly enough, a way to cross from one side of the stage to the other without exiting the building which was bloody wonderful when it was pissing down rain or blowing its guts out outside. The doors had no such luxuries as air locks, so when the doors were opened to let you in again a wintery blast of cold air went through the theatre. The dressing rooms were grossly inadequate if the cast for a show was greater than ten.

Despite all its deficiencies the Little Theatre was better than nothing and to a point, the inadequacies of the place presented a challenge for the set designers who usually came up trumps.

Another of the reasons that the LV lost out to Warragul was that LV already had an Arts Centre, i.e the Little Theatre. Yeah, right. It was at about this time that lobbying began with both the City of Traralgon and the Shire and later City of Morwell. This lobbying would vex both the LLOS and the LTC committees for years, another 35 years in fact, before the City of Latrobe decided that the people of the Latrobe Valley should have an asset similar to that which communities everywhere else in the state had enjoyed for decades. My wish is to live long enough to see our first production in this venue. As a matter of interest a performing arts centre was built in Sale nearly twenty years ago and the West Gippsland Arts Centre in Warragul has just recently had its SECOND refurbishment. At the time of writing our Arts Centre is just a large hole in the ground.

I'm sorry about the extent of that diversion. We shall now attend the 1979 production of The Pirates of Penzance in the venue that was to be our home for the next 15 years.

This was to be the first LLOS production I saw as an audience member .The first thing I noticed was that there were almost enough musicians to make up a proper orchestra. As we were playing in a proper theatre, Barbara may have persuaded more members of the Latrobe Orchestra to join us. Secondly there seemed a much larger and relatively younger MC. This may well have been due to David's membership of Apex, as I, having rejoined the club in Morwell, recognised them as members of the Traralgon club. Another thing that was obvious was that everyone on stage was having a ball. What was not quite so obvious was that the standard of the performance was much higher than I remembered from 1976. My absence from the company in that time may well have contributed to that. Apart from David as the Major General and Max Alvin as the Pirate King I don't recall much of the show but I had such a great night I went second time. This time I actually took notice of the Policemen's Chorus. And I wanted back in asap. The next show had been selected and it was to be "The Gondoliers". White tights again! How lucky could one man be!

## Back on the Boards after the Second Unpleasantness.

For 1980 the decision had been made that the company would do only one show per year and put all its time and resources into that. We had the time to strive for excellence in every aspect, costumes, sets, lighting and especially the music. Sullivan's music is more complex than many realise and Barbara was a perfectionist.

The audition process had been tightened and the allocation of principal roles was no longer a matter of "Muggins' Turn" but how well you auditioned and how well you suited the role in question. This decision was entirely in the hands of the Production team of Director and Musical Director and later the Choreographer. The Committee, as the Producer, had the right of veto, but only once in my time with the Company did it ever do so. The Committee also reserved the right to appoint to the positions of Director and Musical Director whoever it saw fit after due consideration to those who applied. The audition process applied to all. Casting for The Gondoliers was to begin.

After auditions were held, the cast was announced. It appears that two of the auditionees had thought they were shoe-ins for their roles having played them in the past. The female half of the duo was duly given the role of the Duchess of Plazatoro. The male half expected to be the Grand Inquisitor. To his dismay and subsequent ill grace, the role went to someone else. The Duchess then piped up that without her man as Inquisitor she could not possibly be in the show and both hurrumphed off into the sunset to form their own company no less. It lasted about as long as an electrical appliance made in China. However, it did last long enough for me to appear in its production of "One Flew Over the Cuckoo's Nest". I played the part of one of the nutcases. I had two lines of dialogue. I was to deliver these as I was sitting clutching a box and staring and gesticulating in a wild and menacing manner. The lines were...It's a bomb" ...and " And I'm gonna blow up the whole damned world!" I'm afraid that I was as wooden as a pair of clogs and as menacing as a quokka.

That left the company with having to find a new Duchess. They say God works in mysterious ways, as this was how Betty Clark came our way. Betty was tall and could be wonderfully imperious on stage, and being tall she was a great foil to David as the Duke, who was not. David had many attributes but being tall was not one of them. She had a fine contralto voice that could command the stage. Without even trying she could easily upstage David. No mean feat! Off stage she also had a puckish sense of humour that made her good fun to be with.

It was now time to blend back into the MC. There were some old faces from 1976 but many new ones who were to be the backbone of the MC for quite a number of years.

One of the most memorable of the oldies was Gilbert Tipping. When God made the original cheeky Aussie larrikin, Gil was the prototype and having perfected his creation, threw away the mould. He was a real one off. He had the gift of the gab in spades and could be hilariously funny especially when reciting his Stanley Holloway monologues. He was also one of those people that things happen to, which was another source of great amusement to the rest of us. He had the ability to be able to tell some outrageous risque jokes to the FC, especially Joan Blizzard or Patricia Rooney, and get away with it! Patricia always gave the impression of being shocked but had difficulty suppressing her smile as she did so. Anyone else but Gil would have been given a severe ticking off. Barbara once described him as the ringleader of the MC. She may well have been right. His greatest asset though was a pure and profound bass voice. One downside about our Gil was that on the odd occasion he was noticed to have had a glass or two more than what was prudent but we all forgave him. I hasten to add he was not alone in that respect by any means but at those times things happened to him way more than the rest of us. As you may have guessed, Gilbert will further feature later in this tale.

Other memorable members were, in no particular order or importance, were Rob Bronts, Graeme Drought, Geoff Lawrence, Gordan Manks, David Walker, David Mirtschin, Richard Elkington, and more to whom I apologise for forgetting them. Lastly, the MC had an apprentice, young Tony Pickburn. I wonder how he got into the show?

As rehearsal went on I got to know some more of the FC. Some had been in the Merry Widow but I would not have noticed at the time as my vision of the FC was much more tightly focused at that time. However a couple did jog the memory. Firstly there was Joan Blizzard. She was the FC's answer to Gil Tipping. Bluff, straight to the point, and funny. Uttering the odd mild swear word was not beyond her. She and Gil together was a show in itself.

May I next introduce...Mrs. Parry. I think Mrs. Parry had been in the FC since the Creation. In every program, newsletter or any printed matter, Mrs. Parry was always known as Mrs. Parry. I think a reward was offered amongst both the MC and the FC to anyone who could find out her first name. It was never claimed so she remained a woman of mystery. Whilst on that, no one seemed to have ever met or knew anything of a Mr. Parry either. I still wonder about the story there. You suspect it may not have been a happy one. Apart from the LLOS, her other great loves were gardening and knitting. She was an expert and knowledgeable gardener who hosted a weekly gardening program on the local radio. In the down time during rehearsals and indeed during the actual season Mrs .Parry would take up her seat in the wings and knit. It could have been anything but those knitting needles were relentless. Nothing but being on stage could stop them. Some of us thought she may have had them secreted on her person even when she was on the stage. If you ever wanted someone to knit a scarf to encompass the equator then Mrs. Parry was the one. When it came to costumes, Mrs. Parry was always dressed in blue no matter what. She was a dear old thing and sharp as a tack. I enjoyed the odd yarn with her whilst hiding in the darkness of the wings.

There were many new faces to me in the FC as well. Also in no particular order I give you Patricia Rooney, Liz Magee, Jan Inglis, Jan Speirs, Gillian Dawson, Julie O'Brian, Pam Hoppe, Adele Larson, Allison Jones, Sue Thompson, Sandra Jessep, Joy Sim and many more to whom I owe a similar apology as before. Quite a few of the above had landed principal roles in the past, only I was too distracted or self centred to notice, and they would go on to do so in future shows. Several would still be there well after I departed decades later.

Somewhat to my shame, this was the first show where I actually took notice of all the people in the cast other than myself and how good they were. It was also the first time I came to appreciate all those who did not go on the stage but worked like buggery for those who had that privilege and here I will stop to salute Jan Dalgleish, Erna Vallak, and later Ann Haig.

Up until now the chorus were more or less responsible for making their own costumes. In those days most girls had been taught how to sew, so they were expected to use those skills for their and /or their spouse's costumes. Single blokes like me had a dilemma. But through the kind offices of the costume ladies we were provided for; but only after the needs of the Principals had been met. We were justifiably last in the queue. So almost right up to final dress rehearsals our costumes were still held together with any number of pins until our turn came to have them finished .Gil always referred to them as our "Pins Ladies" and to them I extend my eternal gratitude. Like rehearsal pianists, they will go directly to Heaven when the time comes.

At this stage I had not had much to do with set construction and so knew little about it so I shall refer to their efforts later. Who I did get to meet at this time, was the stage crew. These were the muscles that shifted scenery and moved props and opened the curtains. They probably did lots of other things of which I was not aware at the time. So hats off to them. Three I do remember were Bob Blizzard, George Derham and Victor Magee. Vic I also knew professionally as he was also a fang farrier, like myself. Victor and his delightful wife Liz had recently emigrated from Belfast. This was at the time of The Troubles.

I got to know this aspect of production much better later in my time with the company.

As rehearsal got underway, it became apparent that the pursuit of excellence was to extend to choreography. Oh Dear.

In Act 2 there is an ensemble number called "Dance the Cachuca" where all the gondoliers and the contadine would be having a riotous time dancing in a wild Baratarian [aka Spanish] fashion. I was never quite sure whether contadine were the G&S version of grisettes but less blatant or something else altogether. Anyway some optimist thought it would be great, now that we had a real theatre, if the chorus could all dance the Cachuca. So in the same frame of mind that Scott had when he left for the Antarctic, Joy Murphett took on the task to teach the MC the Cachuca which is quite a lively dance with much clacking of castanets. The FC had little difficulty amongst its younger members as many of them had done ballet as kids. Exemptions were made for the more senior and less supple.

It was a different ball game altogether with the MC. Some exemptions also had to be made. Wally Ling was a bit too old. We did not need a fatality on the stage. Gil had a limp due to a hip deformity, which had somehow made him even more of a pet of the FC, so he was out. That didn't leave too many more so the rest of us decided to give it our best shot.

For weeks and weeks, Joy and the MC persisted but to no avail. It seemed amazing that having three left feet could be so common in such a small population of men. In the eventual show the contadine did the job brilliantly on their own. For the men it was a bridge too far. Shame to say it was also the first bridge.

For yours truly another fright was to come his way.

At the very beginning, the scene is being set and one of the gondoliers has a couple of lines to sing as a way of introduction. They announce that they are gondolieri etc etc. The audience knows that .They did read the poster in the foyer! Who was to sing this had not been decided. At this prospect my stage fright reappeared like Banquo's ghost. When the question was asked of the MC we all nominated Gordon Manks without hesitation and also without referring it to him beforehand. Gordon manfully did his duty. When push came to shove, the MC could really be a pack of bastards. His reward was to have his name in the program as a minor principal.

The season opened and the show was a great success but it did not go without its hiccups.

The first one happened early in one performance. Act 1 is set in Venice and the Duke and Duchess are to make their entrance on a gondola. This feat of magic was achieved by using a dolly cart powered by a loop of rope that engaged the said dolly and by pulling on the rope from one side of the stage to make the dolly move towards the other. The Duke and Duchess were to stand on said dolly and make their entrance. The jerkiness of the movement gave the impression of being on water. Of course, nothing could possibly go wrong. Well, one time it did. The rope came undone and the gondola stopped dead in the water so to speak. Muffled words such as" shit, what's happened?' could be heard emanating from the wings. Words to similar effect were also being uttered from the other side of the stage but with an Irish accent. Victor! Such language! More to the point: how do we fix it? The rope had to be re-attached and Bob Blizzard was the man to do it. While the intro music was being played for the fourth or even fifth time Bob was seen crawling on his back across the floor to do the re- attachment. As the set was raised to pass as a wharf, he was not seen by the audience, of whom even the dimmest must have realised something was amiss. Meanwhile David and Betty remained on the gondola nodding and gesticulating as if all was going to plan. What a pair of troupers! The applause after their number was deafening. Also please take bow, Bob Blizzard.

Hiccup number two occurred with the costumes. One the drawbacks of having white tights and white satin knee britches was that when the stage lights shone anywhere water had touched it did not reflect that light. There was a costume change at the interval so any calls to nature had to be made before donning above mentioned britches. The dressing rooms had one cabin each. About fifteen or more queued to use it. Interval lasted only 20 minutes so it was inevitable that some had to make the change before their turn came. Great care had to be exercised to avoid spillage. The second drawback was that the britches did not have a fly. Unfortunately one of the MC's turn came when we were being called up to take our places on stage for the start of act 2. It was not me but no prizes for guessing who it was. As he was rushing onto the stage one could hear Victor Magee's soft Irish brogue, "Gilbert, you've pissed yourself!" As I said earlier, Gil was a person things happened to. As the orchestra was gearing up for the entre-act, there was no time to go back and tidy up. Gil then saw the solution to his problem. Instead of going to his usual place on the stage, he made a bee-line for the group who were supposed to be playing cards and to their surprise, joined in. His idea of playing cards was to get the whole deck into his hand and splayed out in the fashion of a fan dancer in a burlesque. By the time we had to rise and do some singing the heat of the stage lights had done its job and no one was now the wiser.

Hiccup number three also occurred at the start of act 2. We were all in place as planned but some of the members of the MC had actually started a real card game which engaged our attention so much that we missed the entry of the two lead gondoliers whose opening line to ask us how much we were enjoying being noblemen. Our reply, which should have been a resounding chorus of "Yes, wonderful etc", was silence except for the piping unbroken voice of young Tony Pickburn whose solo cry " Oh Yes" rang forth, quickly followed by the embarrassed mumblings of the MC who had woken up. The inevitable chastisement from Barbara came very swiftly after the final curtain. We all promised to be good and pay more attention in the future.

Hiccup number four involved me and the bloody building. As mentioned earlier to go from one side of the stage to the other involved going out the back door and then going round the back of the building and entering a side door on that side of the stage. At one stage in the middle of Act two, the MC had to run this gauntlet. This particular night there were intermittent showers outside. The MC had to get to the other side so we set off and I was the last. It was quite dark outside and after coming out of the bright light we were effectively blind. As I hurried to gain the sanctuary of the other side I tried to keep close to the building to avoid getting completely wet. There were also cars parked at the back of the theatre. The cars I saw, the towbar I did not and into it I bashed my left shin. I was back into the theatre before the pain hit. The fact that tears and stage make up do not mix well together was not my main problem. My shin was oozing a fair amount of blood and one leg of my white tights resembled a Sydney Swans football sock. What to do? Go back the way I came [omitting the towbar] and then downstairs to inspect the damage. As much blood as possible was mopped up and pressure applied, as well as an astringent such a Mercurochrome. If I had thought that hitting my shin in the first place was painful then putting that astringent on it really did bring a flood of tears, Shit, it HURT!!! But it did stop the bleeding. The problem now was how to mask the dark stain in the tights and the clot. The answer was to apply a liberal layer of white stage make up over it. A couple of Panadols and back up I went. I kept such a wide berth around that towbar that I was nearly in the next postcode. Taking the tights off when I got home was not something I was looking forward to but I did manage. I'm sure that stage make up was not the best stuff to apply to a fresh wound even with the Mercurochrome having been applied first. It took months for that wound to heal and I still have a dent in my shinbone to this day.

Apart from the events mentioned above, the show was a huge success and a great deal of fun, and despite being wounded in action I was raring to go next year.

Being in this production had allowed me to share a stage with two great talents. It was the first time I saw Rob McCracken in action. He had been a stalwart of the company for some years but I had not encountered him before. His mellow baritone, confident stage presence and dark matinee-idol looks made for much oohing and aahing both on and off stage. He also had humility and an affable manner. Everyone loved Robert.

Although he had appeared in a show a few years previously this production was where Ian Moore's career took off.

Ian had what is considered gold in amateur theatre circles, a true tenor voice of great beauty and the musicianship to know how to use it. He was one of those talents that were discovered and nurtured by Barbara Derham and Ian was a keen learner. He was to be the lead man for many years and deservedly so. I don't recall him ever hitting a bum note. His rendition of "Take a pair of sparkling eyes" was a show stopper. Unfortunately the vulgar in the MC were sometimes impervious to refined sentiment and did wonder about this "ferny shit" he was singing about.

It was also around this time that Jenny Johnston introduced us to a small volume titled "The Art of Coarse Acting" by a chap called Michael Green. It should be compulsory reading for anyone considering being in amateur theatre. We in the MC regarded it as wonderful guide to follow, the consequences of that belief were to become evident soon enough.

The announcement of next years' show had been made and it was to be a return to our roots as a Light Opera company."Waltzes from Vienna" was it.

END OF ACT TWO.

# PART THREE: WALTZES SCHMALZES

By this time the LLOS had pretty well found its feet in the Little Theatre and soon would be exploring ways of overcoming its shortcomings but this show was not to be one of them. I make no secret of the fact that G&S was what I really loved. I did the other shows because I also loved being applauded by an audience, and since the company had a chronic shortage of men, especially tenors, I felt guilty if I thought of dropping out, and at that time there was still an audience for the European operettas .By the end of the decade this situation was to change markedly.

The experience of The Gondoliers had further strengthened the friendship amongst the MC and this was to go further in the future, but not just yet.

One thing that was a positive was the deal made with the Apex Club of Traralgon.

For some reason it had become lodged in the public psyche that the only show to go to was the final night because by then we had gotten in right .That attitude really got Barbara and David's backs up as they rightly believed that with adequate time and diligence, we would be hot to trot from the first show, not the last one.

So when ticket sales opened, that is exactly what happened. Final night rapidly sold out and ticket sales back- filled from there. This meant that opening night audiences might make up just half of the house. After the rising excitement of dress rehearsals etc, to have the curtain open to the vision of those bright orange buckets staring back at you could be quite deflating.

The deal was that the Apex club would take the tickets for that night and use the event for a fundraiser. It became a Gala Theatre Night with a Chicken and Champagne supper. The company got a % of the ticket money and I think a small levee was charged for those in the cast who, mingling in costume with the audience, wished to partake of the after- show refreshments. For most of the MC, drinking someone else's beer and wine was quite acceptable. This arrangement lasted for many years to the mutual benefit of all. It enabled us to open to a full house, suitably primed with a few pre-show drinks.

Having survived The Gondoliers I reckoned I'd have crack at a minor principal's audition. There was a character named Vronski who had something to do with an embassy and a minor part of the action. I completely disregarded that fact that in this last show I had nearly soiled my trousers when the prospect of singing two lines in an ensemble number was put to me.

Along to the audition I went. I bombed on a scale not seen since Hiroshima. Stage fright became stage paralysis. For some unexplained reason someone else got the part. Probably it was because he didn't near soil himself or choke as I had; had a much better voice than I and he could say, " Madame, your Carry –arge awaits" far more pompously than I could. He was a natural.

Some time later, I said to Barbara that I would rather do my Final Year Viva Voce exams again than audition again for a principal role and that was saying something, as I had failed those exams and had to repeat my Final Year. I really knew I had to do something about my stage fright which was getting worse. I did find a solution but let's go back to our show.

This show was about a row between Strauss 1 and Strauss 2.The music was a compendium of their greatest hits and as its title suggests was nearly all in ¾ time with an odd polka thrown in, and to be really adventurous, a bit of the Radetzki March to boot. I don't remember but I think this might have been another of Mr. Parks' sparkling librettos. The plot is paper thin and the characters, apart from the Strausses, are the usual collection of swooning females, world- weary countesses, fawning flunkeys and loveable dumbkopfs for comic relief.

I'm sorry, but relief only comes with the final curtain. Nevertheless, it probably was a success. If the company made a profit on this one, it showed you really could make a silk purse from a sow's ear.

Apart from Madame's carriage awaiting I have very few memories of anything to do with this show except that another great talent of the future had arrived in the form of Ernie Rijs.

Ernie had it all. Swarthy good looks, charm by the trailerload, a fine baritone voice underpinned by deep musicianship, and convincing acting ability. All this later made him a very, very good Musical Director. He was to feature in many stage roles before that came about. Being a baritone he often was the villain which gave him the opportunity to be interesting. Being a tenor, Ian Moore on the other hand, was the romantic lead who was usually a soppy wimp only managing to win the girl because of the purity and intensity of his love and so he was stuck with this show after show. To his great credit, Ian seemed to take this typecasting with equanimity.

This might be a good spot to consider a few thoughts about the shows that were our "oeuvre". These were G&S and the late Victorian era European operettas.

William Schwenck Gilbert's librettos were first and foremost satires, directed at the Great and the Good, the Establishment, the Organs of State, the Class System, and the pomposities of English society of the times. His command of the language enabled him to do it brilliantly. Those targets still exist today which explains their continuing popularity. Sullivan regarded himself as part of this Establishment, and the Savoy operas, as their work was to become known, as beneath his station as a serious composer. He needed the money though. Gilbert's characters were not characters at all but caricatures of their counterparts in the European operettas as were his ridiculous plots. As well as all the above targets he was also taking the mickey out of the whole genre itself.

European Operettas were romances and had little or none of this satire. Leaden jokes from the supposedly loveable dumbkopfs were as close as it got. These people took it oh so seriously! At least in the shows we did. Offenbach had a good whack at the pretensions of Grand Opera but that satire did not penetrate into the pretensions of the Establishment as sharply as that of W.S.Gilbert.

Our next production was to be a double-bunger. “Trial by Jury” AND “HMS Pinafore” Oh joy unbridled, although there were to be no white tights in these. White sailor pants would have to do.

Enough schmaltz; we were now back with the fun.

## END OF ACT THREE. SO THIS MUST BE ACT FOUR.

In my opinion, and since I'm the one writing this memoir, it's the one that matters, this production was the best show we did in that decade. But I am going to keep you in suspense with another piece of "actus interruptus". As you now know, I had stage fright bad. As you also know I had joined the Apex Club of Morwell within which was the remedy to my stage fright problem. Most of the general public knew Apex as a bunch of young fellas who raised money for charity and did good deeds in the community and enjoyed what we called fellowship while doing it. Cold frothy beverages were often a part of that. I had found there was much, much more to it than that. In those days it was Australia wide, where nearly every country town as well as many suburbs in the cities had one, if not two or more, clubs, whose memberships could be upward of thirty or more men. It had extended overseas to places like Fiji, India, Malaysia and the Philippines. It also had links with other like- minded organisations, world- wide. Membership was open to any man between 18 and 40 of good character. I know what you're thinking...How did I get in? Unkind bastards you are.

More to the point, it also encouraged men of many walks of life to associate together in a friendly environment in which debating and public speaking were promoted and encouraged. This was where the remedy was found. I made myself get into that side of things and eventually I was able to get up and speak to even a sizeable audience with confidence. The fear itself never went away but I had learnt how to manage it. Apex also gave me the opportunity to learn Meeting Procedure and also how to manage projects, especially where money raising and budgeting were concerned. The opportunities Apex gave me were to be one of the two transformative influences of my life. The other was to be the LLOS / LTC but that was to come later. As the 80's progressed my involvement with Apex grew markedly as I progressed through the Club Offices, then District, Zone and State Presidencies and ultimately two years on the National Board as the International Relations Officer in 1988-90. Good as I might have been, I could not be in two places at once, so after this next production I was to miss a number of productions in the middle to late 80s.I am sure that plenty of memorable things happened in them but I was not there to witness them. Anyway back to the action.

As with football teams, our talent scouts had been out recruiting in the off-season. When we all turned up for auditions there were a lot more men there than had been on previous shows. As part of the audition process we had to fill out a form, one question of which was what voice range did you think you were? Recalling David Pickburn's advice from 1976, I put down that I was a "squeeze your cheeks together tenor". An accurate description I thought. Barbara did have a giggle. I think the WUBWT principle might also have come into play here. We had enough men to fill a jury box with some left over to put in the public gallery. A surfeit of riches! Welcome David Haig, Bob Lyall, Peter Clement, Les Roberts and others to the MC. Barbara was now to take you all under her wing and teach you the importance of diction and rounded vowels. Pardon, what did you say? Puerile puns were not beyond some members of the MC.

Bob, David and Les fitted into the MC seamlessly. All had good baritone voices and David, had something of a presence on stage. Les was our version of Neddy Seagoon but with a less maniacal laugh. He was short as his charming wife June was tall. He was always laughing. He had a 'joie de vivre" that was infectious and they were wonderful hosts. The after show cast parties at their place were truly memorable. Peter Clement was a really loveable fellow. He was a bit slow but utterly without guile. He might miss the point of the repartee of the "wits" in the MC but knew a joke had been made and laughed accordingly. What he did have was what mattered, a rich bass voice and could sing better than many of the MC. The extra time Barbara took with him paid off in spades. Choreography was, unfortunately, another matter. Those of us, and I was one of them, who regarded choreography as something performed by others in a parallel universe, formed our own sub-group which became known as the Peter Clement Inaction Faction in his honour.[a nod to the Coodabeen Champions here.].The challenge we presented for choreographers was to find somewhere to put us so as not to be in the way, but to also be on the actual stage. Tricky that.

The stars were aligning for this Production but first a word or two about the role of the Chorus.

Firstly, shows without a chorus are boring except perhaps the operas of Mozart. However, the shows we did bore only a fleeting resemblance to his sublime creations. We got to sing the loud bits which were inserted into the proceedings to liven things up after the leads had done their soppy romantic stuff or after the pages of turgid dialogue used to explain the idiotic plots, had made sleep an attractive alternative to what was happening on the stage. Being in the chorus also gave the less talented a chance to tread the boards to the thunderous applause of their friends and relations who had been coerced into attending. [ These were to be bloody surprised at the quality of the performance they were offered.]On this matter, it was considered "bad form" to suggest that chorus members were any less talented than the principals. Self confidence can be a great asset, self delusion not quite so.

The Chorus also filled another very important but unspoken function and that was to take the piss out of Principals who thought their poo didn't pong. Both the MC and FC or even, God forbid, a fellow Principal, could render this service if necessary. We were blessed that this happened infrequently and was usually confined to those known as Minor Principals who had been elevated from the mob and given a few lines to say or a bit of a musical number to sing. I don't recall any of the Major Principals needing this treatment as it was generally acknowledged that they really were that good. Many of them also enjoyed the fellowship engendered by the MC; as did many of those in the burgeoning ranks of the of the technical and back stage personnel.

We must now move into the theatre for the final rehearsals.

Earlier, I recounted the deficiencies of the Little Theatre and the challenges it presented to set designers and builders. This production showed that these challenges had been overcome with great flair, even genius.

The first part, Trial by Jury was fairly straightforward. The jury box, with 12 of the MC corralled inside it, was on one side of the stage and the public gallery containing the FC and a smattering of MC, on the other. In between were the judge's bench and the various bits of furniture which made up the courtroom. The public gallery was even two storeyed. All of this was impressive enough but the true genius of it all was shown when, during the interval, all twenty minutes of it, it became the quarter deck and captain's cabin/poop deck of HMS Pinafore. Behind this there was an absolutely stunning painted backdrop of ships at anchor on the water at evening. On first sight it was gobsmacking. During the season, when the curtains opened and the lights came up you could hear the oohs and aahs from the audience when they saw it.

All this by a genius named Val Popov whose wife Jenny was in the FC.

I often have wondered whatever happened to that backdrop as I never saw it again after it was rolled up and taken away when we bumped out. Notice how I am now using technical terms. I was really getting immersed in nitty gritty of the theatre.

During rehearsal, even before we reached the theatre, the chorus had been encouraged to be characters in their own right so as to give the show more life. In Trial by Jury members of the MC were directed to react with the principals and not sit like stale bottles in the jury box. I was a doddering geriatric with an ear trumpet miming "What did he say?" throughout. If I was meant to look like an idiot, I succeeded admirably. I also learned a valuable lesson: in this stuff it is almost impossible to overact. Les wore a red and white hooped skivvy supposedly resembling a burglar, Frank Doonan was a priest, etc.etc. Gil was probably himself. The FC were full of stuffed matrons, floozies, hookers etc. Each and every one was trying to outdo their neighbour whilst more or less staying with the script. I can't recall whether the Director could see the danger looming but Barbara, who had come to know us well, did.

Late into rehearsal Barbara had seen where things were going so we were all called onto the stage and sternly told we were NOT, repeat NOT to upstage the principals and to limit the tomfoolery. Crestfallen and sheepish, we all promised to be good. As events were to show I suspect some, no, a lot, of the chorus had their fingers crossed behind their backs at the time.

No show goes on without glitches. Thank God these two happened during rehearsal. As the overture for Pinafore was being played, we jolly jack tars were doing sailor stuff on the deck of said ship. One of these was to stack cannonballs into the monkey which was on one side of the stage. The real monkey on a real ship was a triangular metal object, similar to the frame used in snooker, into which a pyramidal pile of cannonballs could be placed. Our version was wood and not as well nailed together as it should have been. Les Roberts was the cannonball stacker. Three balls made the first layer. Number four was to go on top of them. Number four was also the proverbial straw. The weight of number four caused the frame to come apart, allowing cannonballs to roll down the stage towards the orchestra, to their understandable alarm. Disaster was averted by the heroic efforts of the most unlikely bunch of sailors you would ever see.

The second incident also involved the orchestra. This production was the first I remember where technical gizmos and special effects were to be introduced into our shows. Act 2 of Pinafore opens with Captain Corcoran howling at the moon bewailing the fact that his previous good fortune had turned to shit. Given that this was happening at night, someone thought it would be a good idea if there were to be a fog at the beginning. This was to be tried early in the rehearsal period in the theatre. In those days we did not have such a thing as a smoke/fog machine: dry ice was used. As was often the case with these things excess was never too much. So the tech boys were given the nod to create fog while the entre-act was played. Corcoran up on his poop deck had a birds- eye view of the result. With the curtain closed the fog had banked up to about half a metre thick. Everyone who ever did science at school would know that CO2 is heavier than air. The stage had a slope towards the front so the all the fog had banked up behind the curtain. To restore the desired effect on the rest of the stage more fog was produced. The music finished and the curtain opened and with that the fog rolled off the stage into the orchestra. Corcoran could not sing as he was all but doubled up with laughter. Even a seasoned trouper like Rob McCracken could not maintain composure. Meanwhile all that was seen of the orchestra was the top half of Barbara heroically waving her stick, violin bows emerging from and then disappearing into the murk, and the business end of the bassoon, emitting its usual fart- like noises which were now almost visible. Despite their best efforts, for the orchestra, being unable to read the score as well as being suffocated, it was all too much, so a halt was called. Also, the temperature in the pit had suddenly dropped by about twenty degrees so all the instruments needed re-tuning. The musicians also needed defrosting. Discussions were had amongst the production team and the tech boys also promised to be good and pay more attention to what they were doing in the future.

We are now ready for the show but before that I will introduce two great talents. Firstly will be Joy Sim who was to play Josephine. Joy was one of Barbara's great finds. A truly delightful person, talented, kind, humble, and completely unaffected. She was, and quite likely still is, a most attractive young woman, perfect for the role as well as having a sublime soprano voice. She was to become one our greatest stars.

Secondly, let's hear it for Barbara "Babs" Walker, making her return to the stage after some time away, Babs specialised in the Gilbertian roles such as Little Buttercup, The Fairy Queen and all the other women whose stupidity at some time before the show was set, caused the troubles in which the lead male, Strephon, Rackstraw etc found themselves and which she exposed and unravelled in the Finales. Off the stage she was also a lot of fun but on stage she would defend her territory and if you got in her way you were made to know about it and not do it again, under pain of death. She had a commanding contralto voice and could be quite formidable if the role required it.

So on with the show. It was a knockout. Many a full house. People came from Melbourne to see us! And I am not being big headed, as I was only a little cog in this wheel, but I say that they got their money's worth and then some. All the cast were on top of their game as was the orchestra after being thawed out. The success of the pursuit of excellence was on display. Show after show. Now if you have been paying attention to the recurrent theme of this memoir you will no doubt be asking, "So did anything go wrong?"

The answer, smarty pants, was not much. Nevertheless, one such incident occurred during Act 1 of Pinafore. We jolly tars were lined up to be inspected by Sir Joseph Porter KCB etc. after he had made his entrance. While doing this, a cannon shot was to go off which so scared his lordship he would jump into one of the sailors' arms. This little bit of business was an example of the little tweaks we gave to the original staging for a bit of fun. A strong young sailor was selected for the task [again, not me] which he fulfilled dutifully [despite the obvious temptations].As part of his costume, Sir Joseph wore a sword. One night, as Sir Joseph leapt into said sailor's arms, he somehow got his sword askew to the point that the end of it rose up between the knees of the adjacent sailor. A startled look appeared on adjacent sailor's face. Adjacent sailor stopped singing. Adjacent sailor somehow remained on his feet although his back had become slightly stooped. At the end of the number, adjacent sailor managed to march off stage. Having seen what happened, all other sailors had great difficulty finishing the scene as well. Adjacent sailor went downstairs to examine the damage which was, fortunately, quite minor. A few deep breaths and a couple of deep swallows brought things to rights. Just as well, as I am sure the insurance claim would have made interesting reading.

What happened during Trial by Jury was not a matter of things going wrong but of things getting out of hand. You will remember we had all promised not to upstage the principals. We had also been encouraged to put some life into our roles as jurymen and members of the public. A good number of us regarded this as Carte Blanche to do whatever we thought was funny. W.S .G would be spinning in his grave if he had seen us. Visual jokes on the set abounded and the motive of which seemed to be to make David Pickburn mix up his lines. This was a bit cruel as we all knew that David could do this without our assistance. Not only did he take it in his stride but he joined in! When David made his entrance he never knew what he was to find on his bench. A few examples. One night he found a glass of water with a set of dentures in it. I wonder who was responsible for that? Another night a packet of contraceptives was there. Fortunately they could not be seen by the audience, well not until he held them up to examine them. The culmination of this came at the very end of the season when he found his cushion a little higher than it should have been .What to do when you should now be seated to commence your song knowing there was a whoopee cushion waiting to ambush you? Somehow, in the blink of an eye got rid of it from his seat and proceeded as if nothing had happened. Another win to Pickburn. Another defeat to Rest of the World. All of this was the tomfoolery we were admonished about and had promised to keep to a minimum. Sorry Barbara, that horse had well and truly bolted. Michael Green had a lot to answer for.

I am not sure whether this was tomfoolery or attempted sabotage. The intro music to Trial is about five bars, in which time the curtain opens and off you go. Part of our costume was a small hat which we were to doff after the curtain opened and before we started singing. One performance the curtain opened to the twelve men and true waving their hats furiously. One of them who shall remain nameless but who you have met, had opened his lunch.

There was one night towards the end of the season when Rob McCracken succeeded. Rob was playing the part of the Defendant's solicitor. During one part of his song he was to show the judge a large textbook to show that for his client to marry the plaintiff he would be guilty of "Burglaree" when all the audience knew it should have been bigamy. The MC all thought he should have said buggery which in those Victorian days was a high crime. That was a bridge too far for Rob. The actual book varied with each performance. It may be a text on Fine Art one night or Animal Husbandry another. David never knew what was coming but took it in his stride. On the night in question, Rob produced a large tome which he opened at a certain page and put it right under David's nose. It was an illustrated textbook of the diseases of urogenital organs and Rob had opened it at a particularly spectacular page. While he did this, he had his back momentarily to the audience. The look on his face said it all."Get out of that one, Pickburn!"

The upshot of this was that David now knew what a syphilitic chancre looked like and where it occurs. I never did find out where Barry Johnston got that book as it was not from me. I was a dentist, not a pox -doctor.

There was another time that admonishment came our way. At one point in the proceedings, the Defendant [Ian Moore], approaches the jury box to plead his case. We, the jury had been directed to ignore him completely, by taking up a book or newspaper to read or engage in mimed conversations or just look up to the roof with your back turned. As the season progressed, the mimed conversations turned into mumbled rhubarbs and then mutated into actual muffled conversations. Those of us in the front row of the jury could hear such things as, "Why don't you **** off"", "Yeah, **** off " being directed very sotto voce at the Defendant. I doubt if he ever heard them, which was just as well, but we did, which made it a bit hard to concentrate on what was going on elsewhere on the stage. On another occasion during this part of the show, one member of the jury, who looked remarkably like Les Roberts, instead of producing a newspaper, produced a copy of Playboy and proceeded to unfold the centrefold right in front of Ian's sightline. Being the trouper that he was, Ian did not miss a beat. It was also in Barbara's sightline. Ian had wisely kept himself at arms' length from the antics we got up to, so he made his displeasure known at interval, although his rebuke was quite mild as all he asked was for us to leave out the surprises. As did Barbara, but a good bit more forcefully. She made it clear we were not being good as we promised, although not in those words. There we were, supposedly grown men, pillars of society, respected within the community, behaving like pubescent schoolboys. {and loving it!}

The season was rollicking along and we were having the time of our lives. We knew it so well we didn't a conductor. And one night late in the season, off we went at a gallop despite Barbara and Ruth's best efforts to rein us in. The usual run time for Trial by Jury is about 45 minutes. We did it in 34.I think the cast beat the orchestra to the finish by a short half head. More admonishment.

For some unknown reason it had become lodged in the collective brains of the chorus that upstaging and adlibs were permissible in the final show. When Barbara became aware of this she stopped such thinking in its tracks .Any mucking up would bring shame on all and have severe repercussions. No one was willing to take a chance with the wrath of Barbara Derham. However, at the very end of the last performance of Pinafore after we have been roaring out how wonderful it is to be an Englishman, and as the curtain closes we all pull out little Union Jacks and wave them enthusiastically. All except Liz Magee and Patricia Rooney, who each produced a little Irish Tricolour. Ladies, God bless your little shamrock- enveloped hearts. That was class.

It was all magic. Night after night of it. The greatest pleasure I had was to sit in the wings and listen to Joy singing the aria about the God of Love and the God of War. That vision is as clear in my mind now as it was then. There is still one last memory I have about changing lyrics. At the end of Act 1 in Pinafore everyone sings how a "British Tar is a Soaring soul...".One of the more deplorable members of the MC said that given the history and reputation of the Royal Navy at the time, it should have gone" British Tar has a sore..."

But it had to come to an end. There was a cast party to be held. Les and June's place,here we come.

END OF ACT FOUR.

*Max Alvin and Mrs. Parry. Auditions for* The Gondoliers, *1980*
*A sample of Jenny Johnston's artistic talents.*

# How good was that! How did we do it? What's next?

A reflection on how we did it is what's next. I was to learn over the next few years that the best Committee or Board of any organisation, and the one that is doing its job well, is the one that no one notices. They have the wisdom to let those who they have appointed do their job without interference from above. That is, they must trust their own judgement over their appointments. It helped in our case that many of our performers were also committee members from time to time or even members of the executive. All that being so, they cannot abrogate their duty to oversee those appointees, and take responsibility to intervene should things go awry. It can prove to be a delicate balancing act. Then the Production Team has to have the same trust in those who were on the stage, and those in front of or behind it had to be assured that whatever their role, large or small, it was equally as important as anyone else's. I believe that is called leadership and the people I have often mentioned already had it aplenty. As I was becoming more involved with Apex at this time I was not that greatly aware of what being on the Committee involved. That learning curve was to be encountered later. So all being on the same page was vital and that meant everyone from President to stage hand. And we certainly were.

The second important factor was the social bond that had developed between us. This applied to both genders and not just to MC or FC. Any Principal who thought that the chorus was just there to be the background for them to display their undoubted brilliance was to find out that such was not the opinion of those so regarded.

As you know, we rehearsed initially once, but later in the proceedings, twice a week in the Hut. These were the winter months and the place was as cold as a witch's tit. There were times when the fog would seep in under the doors. We had an urn for heating water for tea or coffee and we did have some small heaters around which we would huddle like Emperor penguins in the Antarctic, but not much else. Ruth Widdowson had the foresight to wear mittens that would not have been out of place in Douglas Mawson's wardrobe.

So when ten o'clock came around, we out of there faster than the proverbial rat up a drain pipe to seek warmth in someone's house where refreshments could be had, both cold and frothy for many or tea and coffee for others. As I was living in Morwell, and was always enthusiastic for some fellowship, it was often my place, occasionally Gillian Dawson's. Numbers and personnel varied but we could talk about how things were going regarding the show and a good deal else as we got to know each other. Sometimes midnight arrived and people had to be all but pushed out the door. The more astute of you may have picked up the fact that I was a practising dentist, so what was I doing getting on the sauce til midnight on a week night? Well, rehearsals were usually Tuesday nights and I did not start work until midday on Wednesdays and, believe it or not, I did act with restraint at those times.

When the time came to make the Little Theatre the centre of operations those who lived in Traralgon would offer the houses. There may have been others but thank you Haigs, Johnstons and Pickburns. It was on one of these nights that we discovered that David Haig was the last person in Australia to purchase beer in large steel 26oz.cans. Easier to stack in the fridge he said. Couldn't argue with that.

During the season such fellowship would occur in the MC's dressing room as make up was removed and costumes changed for street clothes. Because the dressing rooms were so tiny, turns had to be taken in front of the mirrors for all to achieve this transformation with the Principals naturally at the head of the queue,[Bastards]. Everyone was on a high, we were hot and thirsty after being stuffed up in costume and under the heat of the lights for what seemed ages so we did what comes naturally. It began with one or two having the foresight to have some coldies in their cars, which duly appeared. This idea immediately caught on so within a few performances six packs were being produced with gay abandon. Initially this was done with some discretion and since we didn't stay all that late and we took all the dead marines home, no great harm was done. Could we have just left it like that? Not likely! As you may have guessed we couldn't leave well enough alone. The time got later and we got pisseder. Now would be the time to point out that the .05 and drink driving laws were one hell of a lot more lenient than nowadays.

This reverie did not come to an end with this show but with the one after the next. We did get a good run but I shall reveal what happened as we are on the subject. It came to pass that for one or two [and NOT me] a small esky was inadequate. So guess who turned up one night with the grass catcher from his lawn mower filled with ice and long necks which were duly consumed. This, of course, took some time and the hallkeeper turned up to kick us out. Previously he had been quite lenient but not now. He cracked it. Given that, as he pointed out, you needed a licence to consume alcohol on council premises and we did not have one, as well as us being several sheets to the wind, you all better piss off now, take all your rubbish with you and never bring alcohol onto the premises again. That was serious admonishment. Further was to come from the Committee. So we all promised to be good and not do it again.

Sumer was acomin in so off we went, girding our loins to tackle the next show, the announcement of which had sent miniscule ripples of excitement throughout the company. It was to be..."The Gypsy Baron", another Strauss/Phil Park barrel of laughs.

## END OF WHATEVER NUMBER THAT ACT WAS.

This was another of those memorable shows that I don't remember much about. Usual music from Strauss. Usual leaden Phil Park libretto. This one had a running joke in it!! I'll go straight to it so as get the pain over with.

The loveable dumbkopf in this one is a character named Kalman Zsupan who was the mayor of dumbkopfstein or something. Must have been quite a place where the village idiot had become the village mayor. This character had been given a catch phrase which was to be inserted into nearly every piece of dialogue he uttered. It was... now steady yourselves as it will really give your ribs a tickle."Great sides of bacon!"he would exclaim at every opportunity. Apparently his occupation was, now guess,...you're right! A pig farmer! That really had them rolling in the aisles. Phil, Phil, how did you manage to rise to such hilarity? David Pickburn was the poor sod who had to deliver that comedic gold.

Speaking of gold. Here is another of my few memories of this blockbuster. Somewhere late in the show the chorus sings about the treasure they have discovered. I'm not sure if we were gypsies, villagers of both. Of course we wore white tights and kneebritches no matter which we were. We all are supposed to delve into this chest and retrieve some item and hold it up and admire its stunning beauty as we sing "The gold, the gold etc, etc". This was difficult as it was obvious to all, audience included, that it was some plastic or aluminium tat that had been sprayed gold and then had some coloured bits purchased from Sharpes' Emporium sown or stuck onto them to resemble gemstones. Small props needed some work done on its products. An explanation is needed here. Sharpes was a throwback to a past world. It was the predecessor of and was later to become Spotlight. Rumour had it that if you wished to purchase a pair of spats, Sharpes would have them somewhere in stock. The last person in Australia to wear spats was the PM Stanley Bruce in the 1920s.

The last memory I have of this production was that of Betty Clarke as the Gypsy Queen. It was a stand out. She was imperious, mysterious, even menacing. Her performance was what made the show worth watching.

I also made an appearance that year and the next on the Committee. For the life of me, I cannot remember making any decisions of importance whilst there. I know I said earlier that effective committees are those that aren't noticed but really, I don't think I meant it to go that far. It may have been that I had a lot of other things on my mind as I will shortly reveal .One thing it did do was to allow me to get acquainted with a chap called Barry Johnston. I will introduce Barry more fully soon enough.

It was in this year that I had an experience that changed my life fundamentally. It had nothing to do with the LLOS so I will only briefly touch on it here.

My involvement with the international side of Apex had interested me ever since I had been to the UK in 1977/8 where I had attended some Dinner Meetings with the UK equivalent, Round Table.

At the end of 1982 I had heard about an overseas Work Party to build a facility in a hospital for the treatment of malnutrition in children in the City of San Pablo in the Philippines. I had not had a holiday for three years so I thought I'd give it a go. I had never really been anywhere outside of the First World. This was a revelation of how millions of people live on this planet. I was confronted with poverty such as I never had imagined. I saw babies in cribs that I knew were not going to see two more days. I was given hospitality from people who had very little but offered some of it to us strangers without hesitation and with humility and grace. There were sixty of us from all over Australia. I was there for six weeks from mid March until May.

End of whatever number that act was.

We worked hard and to be honest played hard. I still occasionally buy some San Miguel from Dan's and every sip brings memories flooding back. I also was able to experience living in a brutal dictatorship, only I had the option of being able to leave. When I hear people in this country moaning how hard they have it, I recall what I saw and either weep or have to suppress my anger.

When I got home I was an emotional wreck, my mind seriously scrambled but I was also determined to do something about it where I could and Apex would give me the opportunities to do that.

Being in the LLOS was hugely therapeutic. Our next show was to be also.

How could it not! It was back to G&S.

# ACT FIVE'S BITS

As I have been writing these doodles, I have come to admire the prescience of that group of members of the LLOS who had realised as early as 1976 that the company had to modernise and raise its standards. The pursuit of excellence I have called it. They saw that with the advent of colour television and very soon after, the home video recorder, we were competing with them for people's entertainment dollars. Things had to change and so they did. Slowly at first but more quickly once momentum built up. The technical quality of the fare we presented in this year of 1984 was as different as it could be from that of 1976. And one of those who led the way must now be coaxed out of his biobox and into the light of the stage. Now don't be shy, Barry Johnston, come on out.

We have already met his dear wife, the multi-talented Jenny. Barry's interests were not about performing on the stage but the mechanics of staging performances. These responsibilities were the province of the Production Manager which Barry was to be for many years. Barry was keen on any new gizmo or effect that could be used to brighten up a show. With access to a real theatre, lighting plots became more complex and sets could be more elaborate. It was the job of him and his crew to translate the ideas of the set designer into wood and paint. Barry was in the forefront of these developments. He was also amongst the first to realise the potential benefits that computers would offer. Very early in the piece he realised the potential of desk top publishing. On the down side, occasionally Barry's enthusiasm for some new idea got away from him causing things to go awry and when that happened it was only with great reluctance would he own up to his part in it. He also had a habit of bringing as many facets of the production process as possible into his orbit and having done that he guarded his territory vigorously. Later in his career he was to be in charge of the theatre complex in Traralgon, a situation I would find most helpful.

It would also be fair to say that Barry was a polarising figure. Sad to say, but if you got on his wrong side, things could be awkward. However, I got along well with him. When I was on the executive of the company, I was well aware of Barry's faults as I imagine people were of mine but I was also very aware of his talents and that was what mattered. I spent many a night at his place discussing LLOS matters, often after a fine meal,[another of Jenny's talents] accompanied by a good red. Barry and Jenny have remained good friends ever since. I had occasion to visit them in Tassie in 2010 and we had a good night reminiscing about those days and recalling Barry's more memorable cock ups. But I do have to say, Barry, there were times when you really did strain the friendship.

Now where was I? I know. The next show. I am sorry I have so tested your Patience![boom boom].Sorry, but I'm going to test it for one more time.

As alluded to before, things on the technical side were changing rapidly. This included the Program which was once a bifold sheet of heavy duty paper with no more than the necessary information on it so as to avoid wounded mutterings in the cast. For this show, and this is the reason for this latest detour, the cover of the program was printed in COLOUR and had paid advertising within. It also included learned dissertations on the topic being derided, as well as the lives and careers of the authors. Talk about sophistication!

Patience had been done once before, in the LLOS' Pleistocene period. Time to dig it up again. In truth, there is a lot of good stuff in this show. Again the casting was spot on. I was in the MC as usual. This time we were Heavy Dragoons. In my case, a fairly apt description.

After the usual introduction by the FC bewailing their marital status or lack thereof, we get to enter with our swords at the Present!, to one of the best intros Sullivan wrote. Pity it only lasts for about two minutes, after which we get to play at a bit of fencing. It becomes obvious now that the small props dept. really had lifted its game. These were definitely not wooden swords. Wayne Sim had produced the real thing although they did not have an edge. Thank goodness for that, otherwise the season would have been a very short and bloody one. After our duelling, we all emit guffawing bonhomie and then stand around like stale bottles nodding and gesticulating, even miming, responses to the dialogue being uttered by the Principals. They then sing their bits and then we join in and after that we all march off to thunderous applause.

To my mind the stand out performer was Ernie Rijs. Mind you the whole cast was in top form but he is foremost in my memory, particularly his two songs in act 2; one about the magnet and the churn and the other being a Waterloo House young man. I thought the ending was a bit of a fizzer. From being a Dragoon for the whole show, somehow I ended up in the back corner in shorts, shirt and Akubra hat standing next to a BBQ. As Pauline Hanson once said, "Please explain?" There were no white tights either.

I don't recall anything untoward happening during this show, so we must have all been good and paid attention. I expect the customary degree of fellowship had also taken place.

So bring on the next show. It was to be "La Belle Helene." And I wasn't to be in it.

## TIME FOR A SABBATICAL.

After returning from the UK in 1979,I had, in early 1979, set up my own dental practice, and apart from my trip to the Philippines in 1983,which I described earlier, I had not had a decent holiday since. 1985 was to be it; which meant I would not be here for the bulk of the rehearsal.

A good mate and I spent ten weeks touring in a campervan through the British Isles and then France, Spain, Northern Italy, with a stop in Germany. Munich to be exact. I left to attend a Dental Congress in Belgrade before the break up of Jugoslavia and the wars that were to shame the Balkans, and my mate stayed at the Oktoberfest. He met plenty of dumbkopfs there and not all were German. We arrived back home in time for me to see the last night of the show. My only recollection is that everyone was having a great time and I wanted in because the next show was to be my old friend from my youth. My cup was to runneth over. It was Iolanthe.

## BACK TO FAIRYLAND AND WHITE TIGHTS

Before we flit off to fairyland we shall have the usual diversion. The company at this time was flying high. The standard of the performance was wonderful and we all revelled in it. Costumes and sets and all the ancillary bits and pieces had all had the pursuit of excellence stamped upon them. People really did make the journey from Melbourne to see us and we did not disappoint. This pursuit of excellence principle also applied to the workings of the Committee itself.

To keep the membership informed as to what was going on, a regular newsletter was sent to all members. It was known as the "Operaletter" and when the LLOS became the LTC it became known as "Stagewrite". Within, there was a column written by one known as Dotty Crotchett. This was a mixture of theatrical criticism, gossip column and fictitious "agony aunt" letters. It made the appearance of the monthly newsletter highly anticipated. It was knowledgeable, it had little caricatures in it, and it was FUNNY. With those hints you should by now have guessed who penned it.

At this time we used to have a major social event mid- year known as "The Soiree."It was held in one of the members' houses, often at Val and Gerry Kennedy's. Gerry was one of the set construction team which was handy, as he owned a hardware business. Val was one of those we only met when we got to the theatre as her forte was organising ticketing and Front of House. Their house was the best as it was large enough to fit people in and it had a piano.

The idea of the night was for those so inclined to perform their party pieces in friendly company in conjunction with food and some drink of whatever you fancied. Gil would do his Stanley Holloway monologues brilliantly. We all became very well acquainted with young Albert Ramsbottom and Sam at Battle Trafalgar. On one occasion Derry Devine sang Schubert Lieder and our regular principals also made contributions. My stage fright problem had not yet been resolved so there was no way I was going to sing anything, no matter how sympathetic the audience. On one occasion though, I was induced {quite possibly inveigled again} into doing a poetry reading. To make sure that, if in the event I froze I, had the book firmly in my grasp. It was "The Complete Book of Australian Folklore.", from which I recited something along these lines: ... "It was in the Queensland drought, when the colt from old regret had got away, so Mulga Bill from Eaglehawk, who was fed up with the bush, caught the cycling craze, and crying "Murder, Bloody Murder"came down from Ironbark, where all his bloody bullocks had died,etc etc etc."I think you get the drift.

Sympathetic applause followed.

It was at one of these soirees that we heard and what I regard was the musical highpoint of my whole time with the company. Ian Moore and Ernie Rijs had entered the Eisteddfod singing the greatest duet ever written. As you might have guessed, it was "In the Depths of the Temple "from "The Pearlfishers." We were dumbstruck. I still am.

Having been part of the sublime Ian Moore was to be also involved in the ridiculous.

Jenny Johnston had decided to do an interview with Dotty Crotchett as her item and had absolutely inveigled Ian Moore into appearing as said Dotty. When "she" appeared it was obvious that "she" was related to Dame Edna or at least was dressed by the same fashion house. This was to be the final presentation of the night so we had been socialising for a while. Mid- way into the interview, full of the usual double entendres and mildly risqué jokes of which Jenny was a master, a friend of one of our members thought he would join in the action. He had obviously over socialised. It was unclear as to what he had in mind but whatever it was Dotty became seriously alarmed as said interloper put his arms around "her" with lips a pucker.

Help was quickly to hand and order restored as Dotty's paramour was shown the door. It took Ian some time and a couple of drinks to recover his equilibrium.

And now off to fairyland.

I have always regarded Iolanthe as the best of all the G&S repertoire. Its satire is as sharp and relevant today as it was then. I could not wait to don the white tights and accompanying white satin knee-britches once again.

As far as I can remember rehearsals motored along without any calamities such as had occurred last time. We were all becoming quite seasoned performers. We even had a new choreographer. She seemed such a sweet, kind, smiling young thing. She was all of that and then some. Nothing would discourage her, she never lost her cool and her mission was to have the whole cast, MC included, involved in some sort of orchestrated movement. She achieved this eventually, mainly due to her warmth, charm and determination. I think she had the same point of view as Barbara in that as Barbara believed everyone could sing if taught properly, she thought the same with dance. Mandie Black, we who were about to dance, salute you.

After having been severely 'cachuca'ed by the MC in Gondoliers, Joy Murfett had withdrawn from the field of combat in regards to choreography. We didn't mean it. It was just that we were so bloody hopeless. Subsequent choreographers had regarded the MC the way a bomb disposal squad regards a piece of ordnance.

The traditional way of presenting a show like this was to play the Overture, open the curtains and proceed with the action [if the usual languid moaning from lovesick maidens or their ilk can be described as action.]

Our directorial foursome had other ideas.

The overture began with open curtains and an empty stage. As the music began, a number of little fairies entered the stage and performed a ballet to accompany the music and to set the scene. These girls were probably from Miss Mandie's Dance School. Simple but inspired. It was, however, to have an unintended consequence. As these little sprites flitted off the stage, our chorus entered singing "We are dainty little fairies etc". You can use your imagination at this juncture so I shan't labour the point. Unfortunately the audience did pick up on it.

The set itself was another Val Popov creation. The set builders had surpassed themselves .The fake rocks did actually look real, even to us on the stage. The painted grass and ferns looked like you could run a mower over them and the trees looked exactly like that, trees, not just painted wood. To top it off, we had a running stream. Whilst standing on stage listening to pages of dialogue, the sound of trickling water was not helpful to the more senior members of the MC. Remember, we were in tights and white satin britches and Gil was again in the MC.

To show that they had also risen to the occasion, the fairies all had wands that could light up or be extinguished on cue with the deft use of a small switch in the base of the handle of the wand. Simple but very effective. Made for a great entrance onto a darkened stage.

Having got onto the stage, the fairies start having a general moan about being bored shitless since their ringleader got the arse from fairyland for shagging a mortal and in a fit of the sulks, decided to take up residence at the bottom of the nearby creek. In due course the product of that union is produced to the oohing and aahing of our nymphs. It is not made clear whether it was the Fairy top half or the Mortal bottom half that created the oohing and aahing. As it was Ernie in tights, it could have been either or both and I suspect some of the fairies were not acting. Eventually this comes to an end and the MC makes its entrance.

I mentioned earlier that Sullivan had written a great entrance for the Dragoons in Patience, its only fault was that it only went for about two minutes if that. He was not to make this error with the entrance of the peers in this show.

The entrance of the Peers is the greatest example of poncing around on stage ever seen. We looked magnificent in our lordly raiment. Some of you may imagine poncing around as flitting, gambolling or even frolicking but you are only half right. The above activities may well qualify as such but are way too gauche. Proper poncing around should be done in a measured, sedate and lordly way. This may be regarded as supremely pompous poncing and it was that aspect we brought to the entrance of the Peers. At least I did. The challenge was to keep it up for the whole show which we did. When we came to the bit about Britain Really Ruling the Waves, pomposity had developed into full blown arrogance. Arrogant poncing around such as this was a sight to behold. The magnificence of our costumes helped achieve this.

This was the first of my three encounters with this show where the peers' coronets were not made from ice cream containers with sparkling tat and some red velvet somehow attached to them. The first problem with using ice cream containers was that being plastic they had no friction which made it difficult to keep them from falling off our heads. Secondly, being square, there were very few men outside of Germany on whose heads they would fit. These ones were made to fit our heads. Jenny Johnston the milliner, thank you.

After we have stunned the audience with our magnificence, the Chancellor appears and duly tells us the "The law is the true embodiment of everything that's excellent...etc .Certain elements in the MC proposed that it should have been "everything that's buggered and bent."; but what would they know.

The whole show is great. Great song after great song. Joy Sim's golden voice was as delightful as ever. A new fellow named Tim Gleeson had taken the role of Mountararat and he and Ian Moore as Tolloler were perfect .They may have shied at the prize but gee, they were good. David Haig as Private Willis. was the best thing I saw him do. His facial expressions whilst being eyed up and down by Babs Walkers' Fairy Queen were deliciously funny. And of course Pickie as the chancellor with the Nightmare song was a Tour de Force. This show had everything Pinafore had, but with more polish. I cannot remember any glitches happening. Iolanthe was right up there for us all on the stage and off it .The Company had reached a level of excellence that few amateur companies ever achieve. We had a ball doing it so this cast party was something else.

We were on a G&S roll so next year's show was to be another G&S classic:"The Mikado"

But I was not to be in it either.

*Drake, the scissor-kicking butler. Annie 2000*

*David Pickburn. Dear friend, mentor and inspiration. Performer, director and alround gentleman with Mandie Black, ("Miss Mandie") choreographer extraordinaire and also a dear friend.*

*A well-baked ham soaking up the applause. Hello Dolly 2003.*

*Barbara Derham" Maestro and Teacher who believed everyone can sing. They only need to be taught how.*

*Aaargh,Shiver me timbers,matey! That's a fine big weapon ye have there! Pirates of Penzance 1994*

*Laurie Fildes as Fagin. Oliver 1996.*

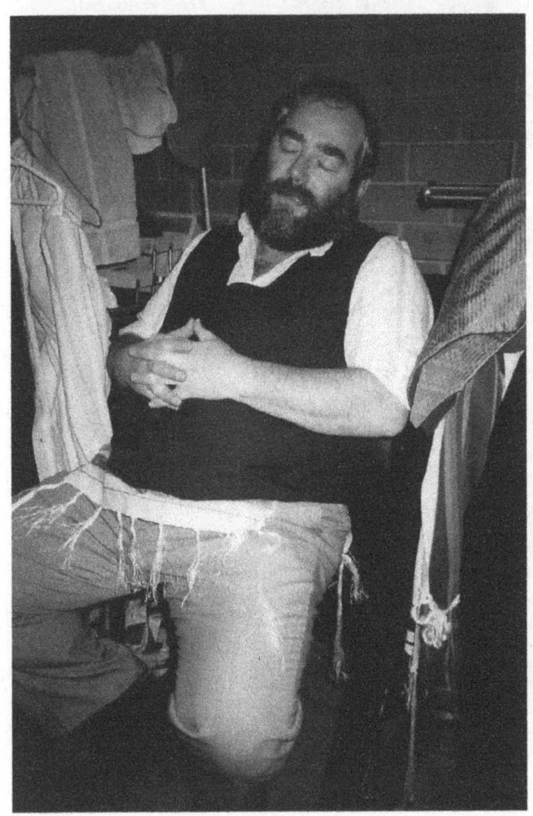

*All that poncing around can be tiring even at rehearsal. Fiddler on the Roof. 1997.*

*Jacob with his mate Pharoah ( Laurie Fildes) at the first dress rehearsal. Joseph and the Amazing Technicolour Dreamcoat. 2006*

*With me guarding the Emerald City, what can go wrong?*

*My last hurrah.
The Rabbi. Fiddler
on the roof. 2008
Mazel Tov*

*The Hut in between shows. The plastic wardrobe where costumes were stored. It kept dust to a minimum but not so good with mice.*

**OTHER THINGS WERE TO TAKE CENTRE STAGE IN MY LIFE.**

# THOSE OTHER THINGS. 1987, A WATERSHED YEAR.

This was a year in which two major events in my life occurred. You, my dear friends, will have become aware that Apex had become a large part of my life by now. The effect on me of what I experienced in the Philippines in 1983 had caused me to devote much time and effort to do something about it, not only there but also in other countries where Apex had been established. I had eagerly grasped the opportunities in debating and public speaking that had come my way as well. I had also now risen to the upper workings of that organisation.

Apex was a four-tiered organisation. Clubs made up Districts which made up Zones, the Presidents of which made up the National Board. The executive was elected annually at the National Convention... The levels below National all had boards of appropriate sizes for the functions they filled. All of these above club level had varying numbers of constituents. Also, Zones did not always conform to state boundaries, especially Zone 7 which was made up of clubs and districts on both sides of the Murray River. Victoria had four Zones, one of which was Zone 12 comprising the six Districts in Gippsland and the Mornington Peninsular. Morwell, my club, was in District One along with seven other clubs. Zone 12 was one of the smaller Zones with 38 clubs in 1988.

My abiding interest was in the international aspect of Apex and had been since my "road to Damascus" experience in 1983. I was always looking out for an opportunity to be on another work party. Unfortunately nothing on a National scale had been forthcoming and sad to say Zone 12 was not a hotbed of enthusiasm for such an enterprise on a Zone level. I was determined to change that. In 1985 I was contacted by an Apex friend who lived in Tongala of all places. It was a proposal from the Apex club in Port Moresby for the construction of a school building on the outskirts of that city, at the Holy Rosary Parish...The school was to provide a place to offer primary education for the local children who basically lived in the City's tip. I had a close look at it and thought, "Yes, we can do that!" Planning began late in 1985 after a trip to PNG to meet the local Pt. Moresby Apexians.

I became the Zone 12 vice- President as well as the Zone IR officer in October 1985.The ZVP was expected to become the ZP the following year which I duly did in October 1986.

The construction of that school was to happen in November 1987 just after I concluded my term as Zone President, as that was the best time before the wet season kicked in.

Being ZVP was not as time consuming as ZP, so I was able to enjoy all the poncing around in Iolanthe.

The workload being ZP and the Project Manager for the Pt Moresby Work Party, made it impossible to be in the Mikado. I was also running a dental practice as well. When I look back on those years I wonder how the hell I managed it.

So the Zone Convention arrived in October and I finished my term of office. Two weeks later off to PNG went sixteen men from throughout the Zone to complete this Project which they did in 14 working days, spread over three weeks. For many of them it was a life changing experience. The parish priest, Fr.Sam Driscoll and I kept in contact until his death some years later and he said that prayers were offered daily by his parishioners in gratitude for what we had done. It was not all work. The Aviat Club and the Car Club were fine watering holes, as was the Dept.of Works Social Club in whose dongas we stayed. After one especially hot day, after putting the corrugated iron roof on, we disposed of 117 stubbies of SP Lager between us and none of us felt the worse for it.

This time in PNG also enabled me to visit my uncle's grave in the

Bomana War Cemetery just outside Pt. Moresby. He was killed in PNG in 1943 at Lae. He was my mother's younger brother and his photo had an honoured place on the mantelpiece in our house right until my mum died. I still have that photo.

I got to see "The Mikado" and enjoyed it. I was delighted to see my old "mentor" Harry Dougan up there again. I was not to know it then but not only did we have Harry but we got the other Dougans and the Maloneys as well. They turned out to be a pretty good job lot. I have no other memory of that show. My head was still spinning from the PNG experience. There was still a pile of paperwork to be done before that could be ticked off as done.

My mind was also on something else.

The dates for the construction of the PNG project had been set at the end of 1987 and could not be altered.

In March of 1987 my mother was diagnosed with inoperable lung cancer. Forty cork- tipped cigarettes a day over a lifetime can do that. How soon the inevitable was to come was a guess. My mum was a tough old chook so she would not go down without a fight. As the year progressed it became a distinct possibility that her time might come when I was in PNG. I thought " Not Again! Please God, not again!" I had been in the UK when my father passed away in 1977 and was unable to return for the funeral. That had left me with an ache in my soul that has never left me. To be away overseas again when mum died would have been a heavy burden to bear. She passed away two weeks after I returned. Thank you, God.

Whenever I was in a show she would get the train all the way from Cobram via an overnight stay with my brother in Melbourne to see it. Some of my fellow oldies may even remember meeting her. She would stay the weekend and then return on the Monday. She once told me she enjoyed seeing me on the stage as I reminded her of my father when they were courting. High praise indeed but perhaps a little biased.

In 1988 I was unable to accompany Orpheus on his holidays in the Underworld. Again it was mainly due to Apex commitments. I was elected to the position of International Councillor for 1988/89,with the expectation that you went on to the position of International Relations Officer the following year. These were to be my final two years in Apex as at that time you were compulsorily retired at the end of the Club year in which you reached forty. The motivation from 1983 still drove me. I knew that being in the show just was not possible. This year involved me in considerable OS travel to various overseas Apex Associations as well as to the Asia Pacific Regional Meeting of Apex and other like- minded organisations in the Asia Pacific area at Ooty in India. The World Congress of all these national associations was to take place in Hobart in Sept.

I had decided also to have a holiday this year, so after Hobart I was off to the USA, firstly to liaise with their hierarchy in their equivalent organisation, called Active 20/30 International. That was in Sacramento. After that I attended the FDI congress in Washington DC, followed by a week in New York staying with my cousin who was living on Long Island. Then a few days in Hawaii and home in time to see what Orpheus had got up to.

Everyone had got up to putting on a ripper of a show. Our old friend Phil had not done the English version so the humour had not been translated out of the story. It showed that unlike the Germans, the French had a sense of the ridiculous. From this distance in time and only seeing it the once, only a few things have stayed in the memory. David Haig in his "balloon" was one. The second was the girls doing the CanCan. Pretty impressive ladies, but not able to surpass the 1976 Grisettes on the pulchritude meter. Lastly, I saw a newcomer named Dave Sargeson cavorting around the stage as Mars. At the end of the show he was throwing little candy bars into the audience. Some he threw AT the audience. I was on the receiving end of one of these missiles. Hit right in the middle of the forehead with, you guessed it, a Mars Bar. Oh hahaha.

The next show had been announced and, swoggle me gondolas, we're back with the Palmieri brothers and one way or another I'd make time to be back in it with them. After two years away, white tights again.

## CHANGE IS AFOOT.

It was good to be back amongst friends again. The apprentice gondolier of 1980 was now a mature Tony Pickburn, a sizeable chip off the old block. After surviving another WUBWT audition I was ready to go. There were a few new faces since my last effort and they seemed to have fitted into the MC with ease. There was to be one big change. We would be doing our last show of the season at the West Gippsland Arts Centre in Warragul. The idea, as far as I could tell, was to play to a large audience which would generate a tidy profit, as well as letting the company experience what it is like to perform in a REAL theatre. I thought it was a great idea. When the time came it was a big day to set up the stage, install the lighting plot and the other technical aspects, rehearse the show on what was a much bigger stage, have a meal, perform the show, receive ecstatic applause, and bump out. In those days we knew we could do anything. It was a doddle. It was a triumph for Barry Johnston and his team.

Something else that the trip to Warragul did was to strip away any pretension that the Little Theatre was a "Performing Arts Centre" despite what the Council might proclaim.

I cannot recall any great cock ups during rehearsals. We were all seasoned performers and a lot of us had done this show back in the olden days of 1980. I noted that our now moderately well- seasoned choreographer had made an impact in her time with us. On top of all her other qualities, she had wisdom. Mandie had no intention of being" cachuca ed " by the MC so only a selected few from the MC were chosen to perform it with the contadine from the FC. I was not one of them. The unspoken message was... One day you all will be able to do this but I will start with just a few of you at first. Miss Mandie was playing the long game. Our job as non-participants was to clap our hands and stamp our feet to the rhythm and cry "ole" or some other ecstatic ululation at intervals. Sad to say, even the challenge of clapping in the correct rhythm defeated some of us. The cachuca was one of the highlights of the show as G&S had intended it to be. Fellowship after rehearsals occurred as per usual. This was when you got to know the others on the stage with you and getting to know Dave Sargeson and Stan Griffiths was a pleasure. Both were from the UK, Dave from England and Stan from Wales. Stan made it very clear that he was NOT from England and so was NOT a Pom. And if we called him that he would display mild annoyance. Needless to say we called him a Pom often. Of course, being Welsh meant he could really sing. One other thing we learned from Stan was that the Welsh made a very good malt whisky and he produced a bottle to prove it. We managed to make it last through the whole winter months.

During the whole season there was only one hiccup on the stage. There may well have been others off the stage but I was never aware of them.

In order to bolster its claim that the Little Theatre really was a "Performing Arts Centre", the Council had installed a piece of equipment called a scrim. This enabled us to be in position on the stage, in frozen action as the lights came up and ready to spring into life when the scrim was raised. In Act 2, we gondoliers were now all noblemen who wore long eighteenth century- style coats. The Act was to open with us all sitting around bored shitless and playing simple pastimes such as cards, ball and cup,[anyone who could possibly be amused by that for more than twenty seconds would have to be a few loaves short of a baker's dozen] and other amusements. The scene was to open with the scrim being raised rather rapidly and the action to begin as planned. All was going well until one night Bob Lyall got a little close to the scrim. As the scrim went up so did the tails of Bob's coat and then the coat with Bob still in it. The emergency stop was hit and after a couple seconds Bob was lowered back onto the stage. Even the dopiest member of the audience realised that this was not part of the show. That did not stop them from bursting out in hysterical laughter. There was no option but to stop, settle down and start again which Barbara duly did. It took Bob some minutes to regain his composure.

Apart from this, our season was another example of how good the LLOS was. Being in it was also very therapeutic for me.

The Warragul experiment was a resounding success and we all said please do it again next year. And so we did with our next show which was to be another G&S . "Ruddigore". I was not familiar with it as it was last done in pre-Billingsian times. I soon found out that a few of us would be wearing white tights in Act 2.Please sir may I?.May I?...Ok, alright. Oh sir!

Meanwhile my Apex career was drawing to a close. At the National Convention at Easter 1989 I was to become the National IRO. Before that, I represented Apex Australia as an observer at the Asia Pacific Area meeting in Feb 1989 in India. I was to represent it again as a voting delegate in Kuala Lumpur in Feb.1990. At that event I was also to attend the opening of a school by the King of Malaysia to whom I was introduced. A most gracious old gentleman. My co-delegate, the NVP of Apex Australia made the appropriate speech. The building of the school itself had been a Work Party Project by Apex Australia and Apex Malaysia. The finale of my Apex days was to be the National Convention in Morwell at Easter 1990, so after that I had all the time in the world for rehearsals.

It has been said that theatre is a make-believe world. We were fortunate to be able to live in it because outside of that world big changes were happening. The recession that followed the collapse of the mining boom, the stock market crash, and subsequent failure of major financial institutions had brought 40 years of boom time to a crunching halt. This was to be followed by the corporatisation, break up and eventually sale of the SECV. The days of full employment, bustling shopping centres and social effervescence were over. The amalgamation of four municipalities into one also caused some upheaval. There was also the amalgamation or closure of a number of small schools which helped to cast a pall of gloom over the Valley. Interest rates approaching 18% weren't helping. Our company survived because of years of prudent management by the Committee .They never lost sight of the main principle of live theatre, professional or amateur: Bums on seats. No bums= no money. Lots of bums = profit. You can do another show. And so it goes.

So let's brighten up our spirits and head off to the village of Ruddigore. This was the first time I had been prised out of the MC to be given a little prominence and I would be fibbing if I was to say I didn't try to make the most of it. It did not involve any singing or dialogue. I was to be a visual joke. {Do I detect unkind thoughts?} The set had been built to show part of the village. That part was the outside of the Mermaid Inn, of which I was the publican whose name adorned a large sign. After the usual musical marital grizzling of the FC, the heroine, Rose Maybud meets Robin and proceeds to tell him how well mannered and virtuous etc etc, the villagers are. While this is going on, I make an entrance, taking no notice of Rose and Robin, and proceed to sit on the bench outside of yon Mermaid Inn and have my breakfast in as uncouth a manner as possible, ending with as loud a belch as possible. Breakfast was a pile of baked beans on an old enamel plate accompanied by a large pewter mug of, ostensibly, ale. In fact it was a mug of freshly opened Coca Cola. I would then proceed off stage wiping my mouth with my sleeve and generally being gross. On one occasion I scratched my backside rather ostentatiously as I disappeared into the wings. Top that Rose Maybud! As you would expect, admonishment came my way. I promised to be good and not do it again. Of course a bottom burp was absoluten verboten. Anyway we already had a bassoon in the orchestra to make those sorts of noises.{Bassoon in the pit;buffoon on the stage]. Joan Blizzard was always there in the wings laughing her head off while this nonsense was going on. The effect was achieved every performance. You don't often get a chance like that to completely upstage a Principal. The trick was to time the burps and grunts to occur at crucial moments of the dialogue between Rose and Robin. As they say, timing is everything! Mary Stewart may have been on debut with us but she quickly got into the joke and responded to my shenanigans beautifully, even the times I got two burps out. As for Pickburn [aka Robin], it was his idea in the first place! Wicked members of the MC suggested that I was typecast. Wicked members of the small props got into the act as well. Occasionally there were the contents of a LARGE tin of beans on the plate and a full mug of fizzy drink. I had about four minutes to scoff the lot then burp on cue. Bastards. The inevitable results of this often made for an interrupted nights' sleep. Still, sacrifices for one's art must be made. I was a bit miffed though, that I didn't get acknowledgement in the program under Special Effects.

The other part that stays in my mind was the scene where the ancestors step out of their frames and after a time Sir Roderic sings one of the best songs in all G&S,"When the Night Wind Howls".

Again the casting was spot on. Ernie was great as the dastardly Despard. Mary as Rose Maybud, the frail English rose and Dave Sargeson as the evil Sir Roderic, stay in memory . With Roderic, Robin, Richard and Rose in the cast of characters it was just as well we were not in "The Life of Brian".

I had by now finished my Apex commitments. I had tried to honour the promise I made to those little kids in 1983.One can only do so much as an individual but do something . I was made a Life Member of Apex in July that year. A singular honour but I think I got far more out of Apex than ever I put in. I have no regrets about the amount of time and money I put in. That was an investment in life. One tangible benefit was that I was now a confident public speaker and debater.

It was only at this point that I realised how intense my life had been for the last couple of years and how emotionally spent I was. I decided to have a long break in 1991. I had not had a proper break since 1988.

Next year we were back into that wellspring of laughs, Mittel Europa, with that well known hit " Frederica".

## NEW SHOWS NEEDED.

I think the decision to stage Frederica had come about in response to a problem that had been present but dormant for a couple of years. Quite a few of us had been around for a decade or more and had done most of the popular repertoire at least once if not more times over just that last decade. We needed something we had not done before. I was not privy to how "Frederica" came to be the vehicle of that desire. Maybe it was that Lehar wrote the music, after all Merry Widow did have good music. Or perhaps it was because Phil Park did NOT write the libretto. Those that did proved they could write stodge as well as anyone, our Phil included.

But the right idea had been hatched.

As I mentioned before, I was in Europe on holiday for eight weeks, during which I attended two Congresses. On was the FDI in Milan and the other related to Young Men's Services Clubs. I had left Apex but was able to attend this one as a member of Round Table NZ. How that came about is outside the scope this story but I am forever grateful to my Kiwi friends.

Prior to heading off to my holiday, a group of us had travelled down to Warragul to see a performance of Mozart's "Cosi Fan Tutti" in order to see one of our alumni. Alison Rae Jones had been a bridesmaid in the 1982 Trial by Jury. She had since gone on to study, graduating with distinction, at the Victorian College of the Arts. She was now singing with the Victorian State Opera in the role of Despina .We all felt very chuffed. Pam Hoppe was nearly bursting with pride.

Arriving home from Europe, refreshed and revitalised, I was able to take in a performance of "Frederica".

From what I could gather the plot was basically about the problems the poet Goethe had with his love life. Heady stuff! That should have had them riveted to their seats. Unfortunately,no.

The show opens with the chorus coming onto the stage, and they keep on coming and coming. The program says they are local villagers. Going by the numbers, I reckon they were the inhabitants of a medium sized city. It was a flashback to 1976 only far more exquisitely costumed. I looked and I looked but I couldn't find Mrs. Parry anywhere there at all. She would have been right in her element.

Several times during the show the chorus would come on and repeat the same song a Principal had just sung. I'm sure I heard a couple of songs twice if not three times during the show.

The arrival and the departure of the chorus put me in mind of the way the tide comes in and then recedes, only sped up a little and a good deal more colourful.

Apart from the Main Principals, there was a small host of minor principals all of whom had their part in a song or some crucial dialogue to offer up. The only one missing from the list was Uncle Tom Cobbley's teutonic equivalent.

The result was that it went on and on and on and on. The music was pleasant in that Andre Rieu sort of fashion and it was all lovely to look at and I'll say now : The dressmakers and costumiers had produced something beautiful that would not be equaled for some years to come.

But there was still a third act to go! By that time no one in the audience could give a rat's arse about Goethe and his problems. As I sat there, I felt pity for all my friends up there on the stage doing their utmost to breathe some life into the proceedings, all to no avail. It was a turkey and it was dead.

No matter how exquisite the costumes, no matter how good the singing, if there is no plot to arouse interest then you are wasting your talent. No matter how hard you might try, you can't polish a turd.

I noticed a number of new faces who would become mainstays

of the company for many years, in particular Christine Skicko and Lawrie Fildes.

Having delivered a clunker, let's give everyone's morale a boost. Let's do a G&S double. Good idea.

After Frederica had laid them in the aisles, we still had the problem of expanding the repertoire. We also had another problem. With the economic downturn in the Valley a number of other, smaller theatre companies had closed up. The LLOS was the only one still active in quite a wide area. Therefore we were attracting talented people from a far wider catchment area than previously. We had a problem that many theatre companies would love to have: a surfeit of talent and not just on the stage. Doing a double might help to spread the love around but really it was not enough.

For me this was Trial by Jury, mark three, as it was for many others. I was reprising my senile old goat shtick, only this time having to use far less make up to achieve the aged look. Other old timers like Gilbert Tipping, Les Hunt and David Walker were also in the box. There were a few old stagers over in the FC adding to the jollity. Jenny Johnston as a madam with fishnet stockings was hard to miss, especially when she draped her left leg enticingly over the side of the gallery. Nice set of pins, Jen. Joan Blizzard as some sort of fishwife was another you couldn't not notice especially when she belted the Defendant [ Ian Moore ] over the head with her umbrella.

Making her entrance as a Principal was Wendy Bradley as the jilted bride. Call me MCP if you like, but Wendy was a stunner. She had IT and she had IT in spades. General and prolonged sighing from the Jury was not acting.

It all went well but there was none of the riotous misbehaviour of the 1982 version. No whoopee cushions, No urological textbook. No speed records. Hardly any spontaneity .We had been sanitised. We were all being good, even Gil. We were on autopilot.

It may have been apt that we followed G&S's first successful show with their second. The company had never performed The Sorcerer before. Now was to be the big moment.

Another convoluted Gilbertian plot about love and its travails which he used to poke fun at society and its inhabitants. Again we gave a polished performance as was now normal for us. I don't recall any obvious glitches. Pickburn put in his usual Gilbertian star turn. I have since learned that David's tendency to muddle up his patter songs had been countered by the prompt surreptitiously holding up a series of cue cards. The fact that no one noticed shows what a clever dodge that was. Ernie as the Old Dr Daly was in great form as was Joy as Constance. The chorus was at its usual no-nonsense, sensible best, all being so well behaved.

One had to be careful at the end of Act 1 when we all drank of the magic potion and collapsed unconscious onto the ground. Having someone collapse across your knee or shoulder really could hurt. I have long suspected Jan Inglis did it on purpose despite her pleas of innocence.

My only other memory concerned one of the props. As a sorcerer JWW needed a cauldron to cook up his potion. To add to the scene, we had a skull in the cauldron which he pulled out as required and when the scene was done, lower it back into the pot. Well into the season, I let the small props lady, Lyn Bearlin, in on the fact that it was not a plastic replica but the real thing. The look on her face was a gem. From then onwards she wore gloves.

We had one sad occurrence during the year. Vic Magee had died suddenly early in the year. He was keenly missed. He was a lovely man to know, great fun, generous host, and never a cross or unkind word.

For the next year a big decision had been made. We would be doing two separate shows .Early in the year we would be doing a smaller production and later in the year we would be doing our usual full scale musical.

The first was to be" The Boyfriend" and the second was to be "The Pirates of Penzance"

A new era had come.

We haven't had a diversion for a while so it's time we did.

Firstly we now had a new venue for rehearsal. We were now able to use the Hexagon out at the university in Churchill. It had everything the Hut didn't. Space, lighting, warmth. It had a little anteroom/ storage room to which we could retire when we were not needed for our particular bits. It was the place where all the percussion instruments belonging to the Music Dept. were stored. We had toys to play with! It even had a fridge! The Hut never had a fridge. The Hut never needed a fridge. The Hut was a fridge! Of course, the MC immediately saw the potential, so little bottles of happiness were put in there for consumption after the rehearsal had finished. When the cleaners turned up it was time to sod off. We were on first name terms with them in no time at all.

Since our President, my old friend from Apex days, Bob Lyall was the science laboratory manager out there, his influence may have had some bearing on this venue coming our way.

The Hut was now solely used for set construction and storage. It needed to be if we were to be doing two shows a year.

I was not on the committee at this time, and so not privy to the discussions but I believe the idea was to have two separate Production Teams. In that way far more people had the opportunity to be directors, musical directors and production team members. It was to be an investment in the future. Unfortunately, some of the Old Guard were not all that keen to allow newcomers onto their territory.

The other aspect of this was to expand our repertoire. There was a whole world of musical theatre out there to be embraced and we had the talent to do it. Of all the shows I had been in up to this point, only one had been written in the lifetime of any of us and that was Oklahoma! and even that was in 1943! The great impediment was the venue. Modern theatres have all the things the Little Theatre lacked. I mentioned this in detail earlier but it was now that its limitations were painfully manifest. Our set designers and builders had employed great ingenuity to overcome these problems and mainly succeeded, but you could only go so far.

But the die had been cast. There was no going back. There was also a far more revolutionary thought being uttered quietly in the background.

## TOWARDS THE TRANSFORMATION

I think it was in 1992 that Bob Lyall, knowing I had been active at the senior levels of Apex, asked me to help him develop a protocol on the granting of Life Membership to those who had given exceptional service to the LLOS.As this had been a function of Apex at Zone level and I had been Zone 12 President, I took the process that Apex employed and used it as a template for the LLOS. With a few minor tweaks and alterations, it was adopted.

Bob also asked me if I was interested in standing for election to the Committee. I told him I would certainly consider it. I was now what you may call a “free agent”, having finished with Apex and also finished two years on the committee of the Golf Club. Believe me, Prima Donnas don’t just belong to theatre companies.

I stood for election as vice president at the AGM and was duly elected. Jan Pickburn was elected President. At this point, let me introduce Jan Pickburn.

Jan was married to David and I had known them since I first got involved with the LLOS in 1976 and also with Apex in that year. The Pickburns were great friends. Each year, for me, Xmas Day began with a visit to the Pickburns at about 11am with a bottle of champagne tucked under my arm. They were wonderful, generous hosts. Jan was also a teacher and she shared David’s love of theatre but was not inclined to be on the stage. She was a very good administrator and served on the LLOS Committee for many years. Her other great contribution was with the Front of House for many years. Jan could be quite feisty if required. If you knew her well enough, you might get away with giving her chain a bit of a rattle in fun but you wouldn’t want to do it too often.

My first task as VP was to update the By-Laws of the LLOS.I undertook this in partnership with Barry Johnston and over the next three years we re-wrote the current by-laws and wrote new ones for all aspects of our activities. These are extremely important guidelines to follow especially in regards to auditions so that all involved are accorded due process. I was on a very steep learning curve regarding the technical aspects of theatre productions.

One very special moment occurred at this AGM and that was awarding Life Membership of the LLOS to Barbara Derham. So richly deserved, and it came with the love of everyone who ever was a member.

Excitement was building as April approached. The Boyfriend was about to be introduced to the world. It was all we hoped it would be. It was froth and bubble and fun. Lots of new faces and vitality. A number of old faces that appeared to have given a lift by associating with these youngsters, were also in attendance. It was Lawrie Fildes' first go as director and Ernie Rijs' first go as Musical Director as well .They were to be the guiding lights for many a show to come. It was also Ros Molyneux's first shot as Choregrapher. It also introduced another bod who was to have a big impact in the future, Barry Whitehead. I do hate to be a nark but stage make-up is for use under stage lighting, not for photography. The program photos were rather startling. Dave Sargeson looked like he had a rather awful dermatological problem.

It was the proverbial shot in the arm for the LLOS. The spin off was that most of these young men were keen to be Pirates!

And so to the second show of the year.

The infusion of youth had a profound effect on everyone. There was a zest about the performances. It was a delight to have been in this one. For fun and enthusiasm I put it up there with the 1982 Pinafore, but far more polished in all other respects. You may recall when we did Iolanthe, a ballet had been inserted into the overture to set the scene and to get the audience into the mood. In this one, the directors went one better. Before even the overture the directors created a prologue with Great Granny Mabel telling the grandkids about her adventures with the Pirates of Penzance. Brilliant concept! Brilliantly executed! That was our first sight of a wee chap called Craigen Whitehead.

Then to top that off,[most of] the Pirates performed a balletic swordfight whilst the overture played. Triumph for Mandie Black. We even had a trainer from the Morwell FC as a masseur so that we didn't have a Pirate do a hammy mid "Grande Jettee". The actual beginning of the show didn't just occur. It burst into life with the pirates getting into the plonk and having a jolly good time. After a while Frederic gets tangled up with a crowd of lovelorn sheilas and that's when his troubles really start.

All the cast were in top form. Pickburn always made it look so easy, with or without cue cards. David Thomas was suitably noble and pompous as the Pirate King, Ian Moore sang a treat, Babs Walker and Pam Hoppe were appropriately bossy and dotty at the same time, as Ruth, but the one that sticks in my mind was Dave Sargeson as the Sergeant of Police. He said to me after the season that that was the role he had wanted to play all his time in amateur theatre. He did not disappoint.

I was pirate in act 1{ white tights and kneebritches again, you beauty,] and a policeman in act 2. And had a ball. Dave Sargeson had crafted both batons and proper policeman's helmets for us wallopers and had also managed to borrow real waterproof capes from a mate of his in the Force .We looked the real thing! It was,however, mighty warm in those capes under the stage lights. Industrial strength deodorant was needed for us to remain nice to be near. After one dress rehearsal we all trooped over the road to the Police Station and had some publicity photos taken with real cops. They thought it was a great joke. Our policemen were all chosen with great care. There was Bob Lyall who was tall. There was Tracy Roberts who definitely wasn't. There was Gil Tipping who was lame. There was myself who was portly. The rest were similarly unathletic. When we marched onto the stage you could hear the laughter over the orchestra! All the young fit men were pirates. No wonder they subdued us. They even had the ships moggie on the job. How could they lose when they had a cat like Fred?

It was a great success. It was probably the best all round, consistent G&S performance we had given since Iolanthe. It was to turn out to be last G&S performance we ever did.

And I think that is such a huge shame.

It was also the last time I wore white tights as part of my costume which was not quite such a shame.

It was also what I would regard as the end of the Company's first Golden Age which began with the 1982 Trial/Pinafore performance. Twelve years of brilliance, with only one dud.

As I was now on the Committee I had started working with and taking notice of a lot more people than I had before. I got to know Ann and Max Maloney and Ann's sister Kate. As well as being the floor manager during the season, Ann had taken on the job as treasurer and would hold that position many years. Her experience of running a business was to be invaluable. Max was into the technical side of things and an all-round steadying influence. He also had a good head for figures. Both were to become dear friends. Ann and Kate's parents were Harry and Jean Dougan, LLOS royalty. Harry was no longer treading the boards but he became program seller par excellence. Jean helped out in the dressing rooms as a dresser and helper in many miscellaneous ways. She made tea for the Principals at interval amongst other odd jobs. She was everyone's granny and we all loved her.

For Pirates, there had been something of a revolution in the field of stage make-up. Up until then we had been using the traditional grease paint, using various tints and layers to accentuate the desired facial features, all of which took vast amounts of Cold Cream or Sorbilene to remove. That approach was now abandoned in favour of just using a base and light make-up. I'm told that the driving force behind this was improvement in the sophistication of stage lighting. Those who could apply their own make-up were delighted with this. It made little difference to me as I had never learned how to apply make-up. I had to rely on the good offices of one of the team of ladies back stage to do it for me. The problem arose because I needed to wear glasses. Without them I couldn't see what I was doing. And apart from that, I was extremely sensitive around the eyes. Even the lightest touch on my eyelids brought a welling up of tears, as did applying Mascara to my eyelashes. There was no way I was ever going to star in "Priscilla, Queen of the Desert". Having a full beard took care of the rest of the dial.

After the success of both the shows we did that year, it was going to be the same for 1994. First was to be something new and frothy like " The Boyfriend".

"Charlie Girl" was to go on in the autumn. For the second show, "The Merry Widow" was to be resurrected. More Lehar music and Phil Park hilarity. Time for a new generation to strut their "Mi Velimo" s. The path to transformation had hit a speed hump.

"Charlie Girl" was a hoot. The vitality was almost palpable. For me there were several memorable aspects. In the story there are four suspicious characters. In his wisdom the Director, Lawrie Fildes, had chosen four of the biggest hams available. David Pickburn, Les Hunt, Christine Skicko and yours truly. My "tour de force"[tour de farce" {"tour de fartz"}] in Ruddigore must not have gone unnoticed. As the season progressed this became a contest as to who could overact the most and get away with it. This was the first time I had ever had dialogue to offer up but that did not faze me as now I was a competent public speaker. Another good thing was that we were not required in any of the musical numbers. No singing, no dancing. What could possibly go wrong? Drying up for one thing!

At the start of one scene, the curtain opens to reveal the 4SC discussing their nefarious plans. Yours truly was to open the dialogue. All had been going well until one night I went totally blank. I had no idea what I was meant to say. All I could see was bloody Pickburn with a grin all over his face. Total silence for what seemed forever and then Salvation! A rather loud whisper arose from the pit bearing with it the words I had lost. Thank you, Kate Dougan. The scene could now proceed. Fortunately it didn't happen again. Afterwards David commiserated and said it happens to everyone. I bet they didn't have his grinning mug two feet away at the time.

The final scene has the 4SC caught in their felonious tricks and a choreographed fight ensues. No one was meant to get hurt. Yeah, right! Twice I got a whack on the head. As they say, once is an accident but twice....?

In Act 2 there is an ensemble number extolling the beauties of various types of fish that go well with chips. Haddock, herring, plaice, cod, etc, etc . In fact, I think by some amazing co-incidence the song was called "Fish and Chips". The 4SC were not in this scene, so when it was decided that it would be the encore song we were rather at a disadvantage. I don't know about the others, but for me there was no time to learn it so when we were all gathered on stage to render the encore I'm sure I was not the only one singing "fish and fish and fish and fish "until the end of the song and thunderous applause.

However the ultimate highlight involved the three main female leads. The story is set in the swinging sixties and the ladies of the manor want to assert their independence and disdain for the stuffy world they were born into.

So they organise a party during which they exhibit their 'Devil may Care' attitude by appearing in their lingerie and dance up a storm for those at the party. You may call me a MCP again if you like, but the sight of Wendy Bradley, Maria Chadwick and Eleanor Handley in bustier, garter belts and stockings will never be forgotten. Even now the memory of it elicits a protracted sigh. No wonder we had hordes of blokes, young and old, in the audience.

The Grisettes of 1976 had been well and truly gazumped.

As the year progressed we, as the Committee, were still confronted with major problems. Firstly we were stymied by the venue as to performing most of the modern repertoire and we were hence limited to re-doing the same stuff every few years. It was also becoming apparent that the concept of a "Light Opera" company was a dated one. More and more it was obvious that things had to change radically. I recall one night when Barry and I were working on by-laws he brought up the idea of using the Town Hall. I was puzzled as the Town hall was just that. It had less going for it than the Little Theatre. I was also intrigued. He reckoned that it could be converted into a "theatre" with not too much difficulty. As he was the custodian of the place, he should know and getting the OK from the City ought not to be too difficult. At a Committee meeting at John Morrissey's we discussed the plan in detail and decided to go for it. One pertinent problem was how we were going to pay for it. In this regard Max Maloney came up trumps. Max was employed in the power industry and knew people at Loy Yang Power who were now running that power station and were looking to sponsor an organisation in the LV to display their largesse as a good corporate citizen. They were wanting something other than a sporting entity. By a stroke of good fortune, their Public Relations man was a fellow called Richard Elkington who had been a member of the LLOS back in the 1970s. In fact, we knew each other as we had shared the jury box in the 1979 production of "Trial by Jury". Max organised a meeting over lunch at "Gaztronomy" and discussions went from there. The initial contact had been in 1994, but the negotiations mainly went on during 1995. I had several meetings with their CEO in conjunction with Richard and eventually they agreed to be a sponsor and a very generous one at that. In a nutshell, that was how they became our Corporate Patron. That sponsorship was to begin with the 1996 season. They were to pick up the tab for the royalties due to copyright holders for the major musical show we would be doing each year.

Of the shows we had been doing, either they were in the public domain which was the case with G&S or the performing rights were held by Warner/Chappell. They calculated the amount due by taking a % of your ticket sales, payable after the season, so you had the money in the bank to cover it. However the rights of many of the more modern shows were held by other companies such as Tams/Witmark who calculated your dues by multiplying your number of performances by the number of seats in your venue and charging a flat rate, payable before they would release the books and orchestral parts, all of which had to be returned immediately after the conclusion of the season. Having that bill covered was a huge help.

Of all the things I may have done for the company, sealing that deal was the thing I was most proud of; because it was the lynchpin around which everything that followed, pivoted. Without it, no change would have been possible.

So although change was in the wind, we were stuck with the Little Theatre for the time being. But a change of venue for the early show in 1995 had been achieved and as Monty Python once said, "Now for something completely different". We were going to do a Musical Hall entertainment to accompany a dinner at a large function centre.

I had decided that I was going to a Congress later in the year so I was not going to be in this Production of Merry Widow. One dose of " Mi Velimos" per lifetime was quite adequate. It was only a short holiday so I was able to return to see the show and put in a bit of time front of house. That was a new experience for me, all part of the learning process.

For this production we had a new leading man called Curtis Bayliss from Melbourne. He was I think a semi-professional and made a few hearts flutter amongst the FC. He also had a great time at the after show party only leaving the party to get the early train back to Melbourne.

Over all the years, we had never used an understudy and had got away with it. Our luck ran out this time. Jenny Johnston as the Merry Widow herself came down with laryngitis.

We were saved by a singer from Opera Victoria who was available and filled in by singing whilst in the orchestra pit with Jenny lip-synching on the stage. No one in the audience was the wiser. This show was the beginning of a long career with the company by a handsome young chap called Simon Hemming.

Just as it was the start of Simon's career, this show saw the final show in the career of Barbara Derham. I sang her praises very early in this memoir and I will again now. She was a Colossus in the history of the LLOS. Nobody had a greater effect on the Company. Nobody was more loved. Nobody gave more of themselves to nurture talent. To try to imagine what the LLOS would have been without her is impossible.

One night I was on duty with Jan Pickburn and we mentioned to one another that the view we had of the audience from the back of the theatre was one of many a balding head and many a blue rinse. It was obvious that we were catering to an ageing audience. We had to modernise. The revolutionary idea mentioned earlier was now openly being discussed at Committee level. We decided that the name of the Latrobe Light Opera Society should be changed to The Latrobe Theatre Company. This proposal needed a lot of work and was to be presented to the company at the AGM in Feb.1996.

It was now 1995 and we had a Music Hall to conjure up, and I was now the President. One of the first things I did was a little piece of nepotism. I asked my niece Jacqui to be Secretary. She had been with the LLOS for four years, doing back stage work, shifting scenery and small props mainly. She was also a solicitor so was very handy with regard to the proposed name change and the legal requirements that exercise engendered.

Putting on the "Old Time Music Hall" turned out to be a bigger task than we first thought. I cannot recall whose idea it was but it required a prodigious amount of work to get it into shape, most of which was done by Ernie Rijs who was Artistic and Musical Director. There were a lot of numbers that gave a lot of people a spot in the limelight which was a good thing for the company. There were however, a number of drawbacks. The stage was minute as the venues management were reluctant to lose seats for paying customers. The backstage area was also tiny. Nevertheless a stage was built that did the job, so well done those men and women. All the technical aspects were achieved to an acceptable level despite the venue not designed for what we wanted to do. Another major problem was that it was very difficult to have enough rehearsals in the venue. The management were under the impression that all you had to do was set up stage, do your one two;... one two;... one two,... procedure and off you went. I think we did three shows for two weeks and we had good audience numbers who enjoyed themselves immensely although they did get a bit fidgety towards the end of the night. The result was a huge achievement for Ernie who wrote and directed the whole thing. The part played by Barry Whitehead as the Master of Ceremonies was quite brilliant. He had the audience from the moment he started.

Despite all the difficulties, it was a great success with the audience. Those of us who had a keener appreciation of things could see some negatives. The show was under rehearsed but that was through no fault of ours. It also went too long. When estimating the run time, the time lost getting people and scenery on and off the rudimentary stage was far greater than anticipated and having had people rehearsing their bits for as long as they had, it was thought prudent not to drop somebody from the show at this late stage.

What few people knew was the problems I had with the management. Welcome to being President. We were doing them a big favour, bringing in lots of paying bums on seats. You would have thought they would be grateful. Not a bit of it. They squeezed us for every dollar they could. They resisted every request for additional space or rehearsal time. I hope I'm wrong here but I don't recall any complimentary refreshments for the performers. And they were just rude to deal with. I had, very early in the piece, decided if we were to try this sort of show again; it would NOT be at this venue.

And so it turned out that we were going to do something similar early 1996. It was to be called "From Gershwin to Lloyd-Webber" but it was changed to "A Toast to Broadway". Maria Chadwick was to be the Director and it was to be at a different venue.

As if we didn't have much else to do, we also decided that we would produce a play in the middle of 1996 .This came about because with the economic downturn began with the sale of the SEC we were the only performing arts company to have survived and there were many talented people both within our company or out there in the wider world who would love to have the opportunity to be involved in putting on a show. The future shows sub- committee said we could produce plays for a short season within a small budget and hence cater for a need in the community. The committee agreed to give it a try. Our play would be the English farce, "Move Over, Mrs. Markham, staged mid- year 1996.

Later in this year we were going back to dumbkopfstein to meet the Gypsy Baron. I was so delighted with the prospect I decided to attend a Dental Congress in Canada.

In the meantime Barry Johnston's plan to convert the Town Hall into a theatre had been developed and had the go ahead from the City. We were to break into the world of modern theatre with a season of "Oliver!" in November 1996 in the Main Hall! We had originally proposed doing a G&S that had not been seen in the LV before,"Princess Ida". Even in its lifetime it had not been seen by many people. With the opportunity to do "Oliver!" now a reality, a long ignored G&S was to remain just that.

The Plan was that the ceiling lights in the Main Hall were to be removed. Raked seating to sit 400 would be erected in the back half of the hall with a biobox placed right up the back. A series of platforms of the same height of the stage would be constructed and placed in front of the stage to enlarge the overall stage area in front of the curtain. The orchestra would be placed against the east wall of the hall. This would also give us extra performance space on the actual floor of the hall. The supper room was to be used as the wings to store whatever "furniture" was needed for scenes acted out on the hall floor. It all seemed so easy.

1996 was to be a big year but we weren't there yet. There were great sides of bacon to be encountered first.

My fondness for The Gypsy Baron was detailed earlier in this opus. It was Lawrie Fildes' turn to be the village mayor/idiot. He did it very well. I enjoyed the show in as much I knew everyone up there and was able to appreciate their performances which were very good. The costuming was a treat for the eyes but with Jenny Johnston, Christine Skicko, and Ann Haig leading the charge how could it have been anything else. The nights I saw it all went well, so if there were any snafus I wasn't aware of them. It was only after seeing this show for the nth. time that I realised I had missed the greatest nugget of humour that our friend Phil Park had ever produced. Actually, I may be doing him a disservice as the joke is so ponderous it may well have been in the original German libretto.[“Who says we Germans have no sense of humour?”.... ”Just about everybody!”] Near the end of the show the mayor/idiot returns from the campaign with a bandage over his eye. When asked what happened, it transpires that he was cooking over the camp fire and a bit of fat spat out of the pan into his eye. Now this is the joke! Tzupan the PIG FARMER was cooking....[now wait for it....] BACON. Oh the subtlety, the irony, the sophistication!!! Phil, how did you keep coming up with them? With that revelation jovial guffaws ripple around the assembled masses on the stage. One or two in the audience may have also emitted a miniscule guffaw and who could blame them when such comedic gems came their way.

Nevertheless the demographic of our audience was apparent.

If all went as we hoped in the following year, the Gypsy Baron could go and give the Merry Widow a good rogering and then Waltz off to Vienna, picking up Frederica on their way and perhaps giving her a good rogering as well, seeing how she missed out with Goethe.

# METAMORPHOSIS

The year 1996 was to be a watershed year. When I was elected president the previous year I was determined to apply Meeting Procedure such as I had learned in my Apex days. If we were doing one show per year a more informal consensus style of meeting may have been OK, but doing two and even three shows per year with each of their individual production teams needing to produce reports every committee meeting, time was of a premium at committee meetings. I suspect some committee members did not like to be told they had three minutes to say their piece and then pipe down. I had no intention of having committee meetings rambling on until near midnight. Nor did I have any intention of the AGM doing the same no matter what was on the agenda.

The first big event of the year was the AGM in February and the main item was the name change.[At this point I will mention that my niece Jacqui had stood down as secretary at the 1995 AGM and her position taken up by Kate Dougan]. It was great to see the large number of members who attended. The discussion was lively as well it should, as the LLOS was a large part of everyone's lives. By keeping everyone to the point, as many who wanted to speak were able to do so. Eventually the vote was taken and the change was approved. Sadly, some members could not accept the result and left, not to return. For those of us who had worked for this, a whole new world was our oyster and we shucked it with relish!

Show number one for the year was "A Toast to Broadway". The lessons from the Gaslight Music Hall had been absorbed and Toast was a well rehearsed, much tighter production. The quality of performance was excellent. The main problem was poor numbers in the audience. Those that came really enjoyed it but there just weren't many of them. One of the hardest things to do in live theatre is to be able to give your all when there is bugger-all audience. I remember Barbara once saying to us that those people have paid you the compliment of coming to see you and they deserve to see you give your best. To do otherwise you are insulting them. To their great credit, I think our lot managed to do as Barbara advised. I loved the Sister Act piece and of course the Anthem from Les Mis. Another memorable experience for me at least, was that the management of the venue were pleasant people to deal with, unlike those at the other venue the previous year. This show was to be the last time Ruth Widdowson was to tickle the ivories for the LLOS/LTC. Shame it was such a low key finale after more than 20 years. You deserved so much better.

We were a bit chastened about the non-success of "Toast". To a point we were under the misapprehension that we were so good, all we had to do was announce a show and the people would just roll up. After all, they had come to see some rubbish in the past. That attitude was to bring us to the brink of disaster in the not too distant future.

Despite the result of Toast, this year was to open up a second golden age.

This began with the play."Move Over, Mrs.Markham". This was to be directed by a newcomer to us but an old hand in local non-musical theatre, John Sydenham. It was one of those fast-paced British farces, full of double intendres, identity mix-ups, and compromising situations that require precision timing and comic talent. With the talent pool we had, how could it have been anything but the huge success it was. Lawrie Fildes, Christine Skicko and Ernie Rijs' performances were stand outs. Success does leave a sweeter taste in the mouth than its opposite.

Whilst all this was happening, committee meetings were occurring each month as usual. At one meeting around the middle of the year, a member of the company wished to address the meeting to air a grievance. He was, of course, entitled to do so and it was arranged for him to come along and have his say. This he duly did and it became obvious that he had a rather noisy bee in his bonnet. When given the floor, he began a rambling tirade along the lines that the committee had been ignoring the wishes of the old members of the company and the committee was out of touch etc etc. In actual fact, to this day, I cannot remember what his actual problem was. When asked by other committee members what, apart from doing three shows a year, he proposed we do, he up and stormed out of the house, loudly slamming the door on his way out. Fears were held for the glass panels in the door. Silence reigned as we all looked at one another asking, "What was all that about?" The committee member who had put him up to it looked rather sheepish. He may have received a more sympathetic hearing if he hadn't turned up to the meeting pissed. I had known our friend from being in the same organisation in the 80's only I was in a different club. He was one of those who seem to think that the more red wine you drink the more lucid, eloquent and persuasive you are, when all that it really does is make you look and sound like a rectal opening. Every club or company has members like that. Always moaning that the board/committee doesn't know what it's doing,{ The committee knows very well what it's doing, ignoring dickheads like them}, always ignoring the ordinary/old /floor members while they, the committee, are all on a big ego trip. These bods never stand for executive positions at the AGM, as that would involve them in running the organisation and TAKING RESPONSIBILITY for the result and having their capabilities or lack thereof, subject to scrutiny. No way are they going to expose themselves to criticism. They may stand for committee and their motive for standing is, not to actually offer some expertise, but to "Stick a rocket up 'em" or" stir them up" etc or because they are "ignoring the ordinary/old/ etc etc." You get the idea.

I supposed he brightened up an otherwise dreary winter's night of working out how we were to produce successful shows.

The Great Theatrical Experiment that was to be Oliver! was now approaching.

As I was now the President of the company I had to perform what was to be a ritual for all incoming presidents for the next twenty years and that was to make a submission to the Council for the erection of a proper Performing Arts Centre. I had been made aware that, with an election coming up soon, the State government had made it known that if the Council was to request funding, it would be looked on favourably. All that was needed was a definite commitment and selection of location. So a delegation, led by myself and David Pickburn, met with council to make our case. David did it with all the eloquence he had but it was to no avail. Apart from a couple of councillors, our arguments met with complete indifference. The stupid, infantile bickering between the towns as to which was to be the location torpedoed any chance of it happening. There was even one councillor who persisted with his fantasy that the University out at Churchill should be considered as they had made noises to him in that direction. With the centre of population being Traralgon, with the "Performing Arts Centre" already there and hence a site already with infrastructure in place, where else would anyone with even half a brain put it.

The above-mentioned University was known as Monash Gippsland. It is now known as Federation University. And that was what the council basically said to us. There may have been usual glazing over of eyes as David and I spoke but there was no closing of minds. They were never open in the first place. For the majority of our beloved councillors, if brains were dynamite, the explosion wouldn't ruffle a hair. But what would I know, I was only a ratepayer.

# TRIUMPH

The preparations for Oliver were under way as soon as the AGM ended despite our immediate attention being focused on "Toast to Broadway". I can reveal now that the Loy Yang sponsorship would have been a good deal harder to get had the proposed name change not happened.

We were in a bind though. With "Toast" costing us rather than bringing in money, it left us with a problem finding the rather large sum required to pay the royalties for the rights to Oliver!, as well as funding the production "Move Over Mrs.Markham". As I mentioned earlier that money needed to be paid before they would send the music. We knew that the money from Loy Yang would be forthcoming but there was a hiatus in the time line where writing a large cheque might have been embarrassing. This problem was overcome by a number of the Committee putting their hands in their own pockets to tide the company over. Very few people knew of this. I thank and salute them!

With the passing of the year, there was genuine excitement about how different this show would be to everything that preceeded it. Being able to use the equivalent of three stages made the directors almost quiver with excitement. We had a new musical director in David Williams who was Happy to be known as Grumpy.[ He certainly wasn't Dopey, although, deep down, he may well have been quite Bashful]. Why, I was never able to work out. I always found him to be quite a friendly, pleasant man to deal with. Miss Mandie had all this space for the crowd to dance in without the risk of knocking sets over or tumbling into the pit. It was not a breath of fresh air that was blowing through the company but a force ten gale and it was so exhilarating.

The choice of "Oliver!" had been a wise one. If you want full houses, put on a show with lots of kids. Kids have parents, siblings, grandparents, uncles, aunties, schoolmates all of which have a bum to put on a seat. However much that may have been the case, you still needed to put on a quality show. It was hard work but we could all see that this was going to be something great. The energy brought by all the youngsters was infectious and what a talented lot they were. Teaching kids to perform on stage was right up David and Mandie's alley. The four leads, Gavin Rode and Christopher Larsen as Olivers, and Amy Larsen and Melissa Barnes as Artful Dodgers were all brilliant. The rest of the cast were spot on. Lawrie Fildes as Fagin was also top class. There was a newcomer called Andrew Broadbent who played Bill Sykes and was a scary piece of work. I'm quite sure Ian Moore was delighted to play something other than a love- forsaken victim of other peoples stuff ups. There were also a number of youngsters in the chorus who were to feature prominently in later years. For example, Glenn Ross, Nick Kong, Kim Smith, Ben Jenner, Brooke Soutar and Jessica Byers. There were plenty of lesser roles for those not so brilliant and we all did our bit to make the show a success. I had the role of Mr.Brownlow. It was the first time I had a named part so technically I was a PRINCIPAL! No singing, no dancing, a good bit of dialogue though, and ...[ be still my beating heart !]...A photo in the program AND a photo in the theatre foyer!!! Whoopee I've hit the big time! I can now strut around as if my poo doesn't pong like I've seen too many other MINOR principals do.

It was also the first time I'd had the opportunity to be able see my way clearly around the stage. Ever since the age of fifteen I had needed to wear glasses as I was short-sighted and had astigmatism. It has been only recently that I have had to use glasses to read papers or books. But I had great trouble with distance vision without them. Besides, given that all the shows we had been doing were all set in some time in the past, a pair of modern specs would look so out of place. [Refer to the cover of the program for "Oliver!"].The exception had been Charlie Girl.

Up until this time our sets had been quite simple and usually static and so relatively easy to negotiate when going on and off the stage, even more so when I was usually stuck up the back of the stage, out of the way with the rest of the Inaction Faction. The one great exception had been the babbling brook in "Iolanthe". Otherwise getting off the stage was simple. You aimed for the nearest gap in the scenery or between the flats and led the charge. You had, of course to make sure that the gap you chose was an actual exit. It did not do to go for the gap that was blocked with the curtain ropes. The stage crew did not appreciate you getting tangled up in them as they were trying to close them. When you had difficulty seeing the gaps, it all became a bit of a gamble. I mentioned this to my optometrist during a routine examination. After he had finished the examination, he went into his office and came out with an old pair of gold wire frames that he had found in a box when he bought the practice. They looked just like the glasses in the most well-known picture of Franz Schubert. He was able to put some lenses in them and voila! I could now ponce around the stage and see where I was going. The downside was that I could now see the audience. Before this, they had been just a blurry mass.

One of the fondest memories I have of Oliver!, was seeing the sign outside the theatre saying....FULL HOUSE. For us on the Committee, O, Joy Unbounded!

There was a downside to having the show in the modified Hall. For a number of years we had used the Final Dress Rehearsal as a Preview Performance for the residents of the Retirement and Old folks' homes who were ambulant, at no cost to them. The Homes' Mini buses would arrive and the passengers were off-loaded with their walking frames and such like and assisted to their seats by our kind and efficient front-of- house people. It did take some time to have them all comfortable and all the walkers correctly labelled and parked in the passageway outside of the theatre proper but still on the premises. The order of parking them needed to be able to be done in reverse order when it came to leaving. If not there would be chaos. Our lot had it down pat. I hasten to add that this rehearsal occurred on an afternoon before we opened, not at night. The old folks loved it and we loved having them. The logistics of the Hall modification did not allow us to do all this, which was a shame.

This was also the last time we took a show to Warragul for a one-off performance. The logistics were just too difficult. We really should have known that beforehand. I still have vivid memories of all the kids running around the big wide stage at the rehearsal seemingly oblivious to the unguarded drop at the front of the stage into the orchestra pit. I had visions of some youngster being skewered by a violin bow. Fortunately no such accidents occurred.

All the risks, all the work, all the vision; vindicated.

Because we were not in the greatest shape initially to finance the show we had to apply strict budgetary discipline. This, of course, should apply to each and every production. Later when we were in a good financial position, this was overlooked with the inevitable consequences. Putting the show in the modified main hall also caused costs to rise dramatically. Firstly the rent of the venue was substantially greater and the acoustic of the hall was poor so that the principals had to wear mikes. The hire of those also added a sizeable sum to the costs. Although budgets are calculated on having a moderate percentage of the house filled, to have some full houses was a necessity. This year was the one where Barry Johnston was finally convinced that he could not physically fulfil the role of Production Manager for three shows simultaneously. Other people who had the expertise were at hand and they needed to be given the reins.

It was a huge success but it was just a beginning. 1997 was to bring the greatest show we ever did. We also had the good sense to do only two shows that year. Having done three this year, the workload had been brutal. And I was still running a busy dental practice.

Time for a wee diversion.

In September of 1996, something totally unrelated to, but way more important than the theatrical world, was afoot. There was a proposal that VFL Clubs Melbourne and Hawthorn should merge! The Horror!!! So a carload of us Demons supporters, Peter Larsen, David Pickburn and myself and one other whose name I can't recall, went down to Melbourne on the night it was to be voted on and joined the crowds to prevent this. It was an exciting night. The merger did not occur due to Hawthorn members voting NO. Passions were high. On the way home after passions had cooled a bit, I felt a bit uneasy about having been part of the mob who heckled and shouted down a person who, over the years, had given his all for the MFC, Ian Ridley. Even if you are in the right, mob psychology can be a scary thing. You may ask, what did all that have to do with culture, and my reply, having been born and raised a Victorian, is: everything.

Now back to the LTC.

The AGM had brought a couple of new faces to the Committee, one of whom was actually an old face, our friend Gilbert Tipping. This was to be his last hurrah as his hip problem has precluded him from being on the stage but he was keen to be still part of the company. The MC was to be a different place without him. Gilbert, you were such a loveable rogue to have around.

Not long after the AGM, one of our most stalwart members passed away after a long illness, that being George Derham, Barbara's husband. George was the archetype of the laconic Australian man on the land. He was a wonderful support for Barbara in all her interests. He was as quiet as Barbara was effervescent. He was one of that great group of set-builders and stage crew that allowed us to do our stuff on such great sets year in year out. A lovely man and his passing was felt keenly.

Bursting with confidence, we set out to produce another English farce, "Noises Off". John Sydenham was again the Director. For this show we had a new Production Manager in Le-anne McCraw. The original idea for these plays was for them to be simple but not too simple a set, but not de Mille extravaganzas either. It turned out that this set was more de Mille than Becket, so your stage manager had to be on the ball. When I first saw the set with all its' scaffolding, I thought for one brief moment that the Council had actually started on building a real Arts Centre, but sorry, no such luck. With all those doors and stairs, the cast had to be fit as well! We also had two more actors from the non-musical world in Beth and Jack Millar to compliment our own talented troupe.

It was a brilliant success. It played to full Houses [Hooray!!!]. I admit that I was not a great play goer but this changed that attitude. I loved it every time I saw it and laughed until crying often. Apart from the usual suspects such as Ernie, Christine and Lawrie, Darren Hunt stood out. Darren was the scion of Les who had been part of the company since the Mesozoic era.

We were to do a number of these plays and although they all had their merits and generally were successful,"Noises Off" was, to me, the pick of them.

After the success of Noises Off, we had a full head of steam and a great deal of confidence to tackle "Fiddler on the Roof."

The set designers and builders excelled themselves. All areas available were used. In the area behind the curtain, they had built Tevye's house .You could have almost lived in it yourself! The front opened out to reveal a room with furniture and all. No minimalist rubbish here! When Tevye spoke about there being a fiddler on the roof in the prologue, we actually had a fiddler on the roof of the house playing the fiddle. Authenticity was the watchword.

Great efforts were made by the directing team to get as accurate as possible, a picture of Jewish life at the time and place. We all had to think of ourselves as those people. Things were explained to us as to the ceremonies and the general way of thinking. The costumes were vetted by our Jewish advisor as to their authenticity. We were to become Jewish for the three hours we were on the stage.

Every member of the cast was perfect for their role, right down to the youngest of the kids. We had a newcomer for Tevye in John Black, who had previously played the role at Warragul. He had been born to play that part. Topol was world famous for his portrayal of Tevye. John was not far behind him.

I won't name everyone else because every one of them was brilliant. Having just said that, her portrayal of "Golde" was the best thing I ever saw Pam Hoppe do. There are many, many memories of this show and I wish to share them because being in that show was another life changing experience which is another reason why my love for the LLOS /LTC is visceral.

Late in the rehearsal period when we were in the hall, one Saturday or Sunday afternoon it had become very hot in the hall due to it being unseasonably warm outside and having had the stage lights on for a while when there was this almighty crack that echoed around the hall, to cries of "Shit! What was that?" "That" was the noise made by the back of the double bass splitting in half. "Grumpy" the MD, being a double bass player himself, had a look of horror on his face as if his nearest and dearest had just been shot. He seemed to take it as a personal insult from the Almighty to have such a thing happen to a double base and we, having created such a hothouse, were equally to blame. He really did his nut! It took quite a while to settle him down.

We had not budgeted for the cost of repairs to musical instruments as I'd never heard of it happening before. The uncertainties of live theatre! In due course the instrument was repaired and another was obtained for the season. Many a prayer was uttered that such a disaster would not be repeated during a performance.

We were as rehearsed as well as possible and so welcome to Anatevka.

As the lights dimmed and the introductory music played, a change occurred. The audience ceased to be an audience. They became visitors to our schtetl of Anatevka. They were to come with us on an emotional journey that few of them expected. We also were to go an equally emotional journey ourselves. We introduced them to our "Tradition!". The first half of the show has great comedy. The wry humour of "If I was a rich man" made it a world- wide hit. To listen to John sing it in our show was to learn why.

Then the whole atmosphere changed with the Sabbath Prayer.

We were gathered together in our family groups. At the end of it, complete silence and then heartfelt applause. We and the audience were as one.

The next scenes in the tavern were a huge contrast. Jovial and lighthearted but with a touch of menace at the end. Here I will salute Mandie Black's triumph. In this scene there is quite a vigorous dance done by the men as they sing L'Chaim. I was in it and did not screw up once. I had climbed my choreographic Everest. After more than twenty years!!

The Dream sequence was Joy Sim's to own. To think she was once such a sweet young Josephine, and now a screeching banshee.[ Yes, I know Banshees are Irish folklore but you get the idea].

Act 1 ends with the wedding in Tevye's yard. "Sunrise, Sunset" had the audience in tears. You could hear them. We tried to have the actual wedding ceremony as authentic as possible even to the breaking of the glass. Our Jewish advisor approved which made us all feel elated. Then the mood is changed with the famous Bottle Dance. Ernie, Barry, Simon had everyone gasping in amazement. We had watched them at rehearsal going through it time after time after time and were always impressed. I still am. Huge applause from the audience. All is going well, even the Rabbi has got into the act, until the Russian Cops turn up and proceed to wreck the place. Authenticity reigned. People were pushed about, tables and chairs overturned, plates smashed. You could hear cries of 'Oh" and "No" from the audience as each act of violence occurred. The stage crew had quite a job cleaning up over the interval. We did have to tone it down a bit as things did threaten to get out of hand.

At the start of Act 2 all seems to be going as normal for the people of Anatevka but as you know, this was not to last. The first couple of scenes set the scene for the disaster that was to fall on all in Anatevka. The scene where Tevye's second daughter is waiting for the train to take her to her man Perchik in Siberia was riveting. It was as if John and Emmy were actual father and daughter. Heart- rending. The tears fell like rain in the audience. There were quite a few off- stage as well.

How they did that scene every performance and not lose composure was a miracle, and there was more to come.

There is some momentary lightheartedness when Motel shows off his new sewing machine, but we know that will not be for long.

Of all the scenes in the show, the next sequence has the greatest punch. It happens when Chava tells her father that she wants to marry outside the Faith.[We were offstage in the adjacent supper room during this sequence. Ernie was watching the CCTV getting ready for us to sing from there}. This, of course, is a step Tevye cannot condone. It is anathema to him. As this sequence progresses, the atmosphere in the hall is electric. Then at the moment Tevye disowns his daughter we all sing Tradition! three times. When I sang it I could feel the hairs on the back of my neck stand up. And when she cries out "Papa, Papa!" as he leaves her, the sobbing in the audience could be heard back stage. Heart breaking! We were not finished with them yet.

The final scene when the people have been given the order to leave and their singing about their schtetl Anatevka, did little to lift the mood until someone opines that really, Anatevka was a dump and we really would be better off someplace else. The final scene had us proceeding from the offstage left at floor level in the supper room, ascend the steps up to the stage proper, pass Tevye's house and continue off stage right into the adjacent Little Theatre. This was done without set dialogue as the music played. We were encouraged to have the occasional word to the various children as any family would do. Again everyone's emotions were put through the wringer. When each group arrived into the Little Theatre stage we were all in tears ourselves especially on the final night. In another piece of directorial brilliance, the last villager to depart was Nahum the beggar. Tracy Roberts had the stage to himself for a couple of minutes as he looked about him, and into Tevye's house to see if there was anything worth taking .All this was done as the music faded and the last one off, playing his own music was the Fiddler. Total silence reigned for some moments before the audience dared breathe again and then heartfelt and deserved applause. Then came the encore.

Often when “Fiddler “is produced, “If I were a rich man” is sung as the encore so the audience goes away in a happy frame of mind. Not with us. Our directors chose the Sabbath Prayer to be our farewell piece. It just felt more fitting.

We were to have the privilege of doing that many times and often to full houses. We had many a visitor from Melbourne and beyond come to see us.

And I had the privilege of having that triumph occur on my watch as President. I was never more proud of our company.

In 2002, I was in Europe to attend the FDI Congress in Vienna. As part of my travels, I decided to visit the countries of central Europe which included Krakow in Poland. Not far from there is a place of eternal infamy. Its name in German is Auschwitz. I spent a day there. When my memories of “Fiddler” collided with the reality of the Holocaust, it was a most unsettling experience. Suffice to say that if anyone tells you that vodka does not give you a hangover they are talking rubbish.[ Why vodka? I was in Poland! And they say they, not the Russians, invented the stuff and who was I to argue?] Sadly, we had to bid “The Fiddler” good-bye.

We had three shows coming up for 1998 and production for the first was already under way. With Oliver! we had tapped into a wealth of young talent which, apart from school productions had no outlet to perform. David Pickburn proposed that we produce a show specifically for a junior cast and even for stage crew and assistant directors. The committee readily agreed and “Open Season” was born. We also regarded it as a training facility for our future. It was to have a short season in the Little Theatre and a restrained budget. Although the cast were juniors they had the artistic, financial and technical backing of the LTC.

I went only the once and enjoyed seeing all those youngsters doing their stuff but to my embarrassment I can’t recall much else about it at this distance. The second show was to be a play by David Williamson called “Money and Friends”

Before we get to that, I had the great pleasure to announce at our

AGM that David Pickburn, Harry Dougan and Barry Johnston were our newest Life Members. David and Barry have featured a fair bit in this chronicle so their cases may be obvious but Harry was from way back in the Jurassic Period as a founding member of the LLOS in 1963, and his great contribution was before the time of most of us. All three were richly deserved.

"Money and Friends" was a bit different from its two predecessors as it was not the typical farce as they had been and so its comedy was more in its dialogue and characters. Again John Sydenham directed. I am willing to acknowledge that I am not the most learned when it comes to theatre. I am of the school that goes to the theatre to be entertained. I really have no great desire to be challenged. Daily life provides enough of that. So the cerebral humour of "Money and Friends" left me rather indifferent. I am quite sure that many other people saw it differently to me. With hindsight, I think I was entering a period of burn out at this stage. Presiding over three shows and all the other presidential obligations was, in conjunction with running a dental practice, taking its toll on me. I decided not to audition for "My Fair Lady". I had not had a holiday since 1995. The FDI Congress was in Barcelona that year, so I decided that I would attend. I would be able to be back in time to see the show.

However, we made the decisions about the shows for 1999. As "Open Season" had gone well, we decided to do another junior show. It was to be "Macbeth, the Rock Opera" to be staged in the Little Theatre. In hindsight the last two words "Rock Opera" should have rung a few alarm bells. I mentioned way back in the introduction that some descriptions should automatically raise the alarm, Folk Mass and Rock Opera are two of those. We were to do another play, "Lend me a Tenor", and the major musical, "Follies" by Stephen Sondheim. How those choices came about was to be a topic of debate that has not settled yet.

When I left for my holiday in early September all seemed to be going well so I left them to it.

My ultimate destination was Barcelona but I spent some weeks travelling from Zurich where I landed, to the UK, and back to France and to Northern Spain by way of a Eurail Pass. I was really enjoying the break. Provincial France at that time of year is delightful. I was able to give my trusty, rusty French another outing. Things started to go awry when I got to Santiago de Compostela. I had had a sore left ear for a week or so and it was not getting better so I went to a hospital clinic and they gave me some antibiotic drops. I went back to my hotel and proceeded to put some into my ear. Immediately I did so, it was if a switch had been flicked. I went totally deaf in that ear. I was not to regain hearing in that ear for over 6 months. Before I eventually arrived in Barcelona, I had the opportunity to experience that most iconic specimen of Spanish theatre. I attended the bullring in Zaragossa. Having read Hemingway's "Death in the Afternoon" I had some idea of how it should be done. I was fascinated. The blood did not bother me; after all I had been a practising dentist for twenty years!

Whilst I was in Barcelona, I decided that I would not stand for election the next year.

I realised that I had had it. I was spent. I was also getting a lesson on the difficulties deaf people face each and every day.

I arrived home in time for the last weekend of the show. I had a couple of days to shake off the jet lag first.

As I had not been in the cast for this show, I did not have same emotional investment in it as I had had in Oliver! and Fiddler That is not to say that it was any less of the triumph it most certainly was. It was wonderful. Again the casting was spot on with some great performances from Emmy Coleman in the title role, Lawrie Fildes as Alfred Doolittle, Ernie as Higgins and Jim Evans as Pickering. Jim was returning to the company after more than twenty years away. He had been a very dedicated member back in the pre-Billingsian era. If he had been in the 1976 Merry Widow, I'm afraid I did not recall it.

The dancing by the MC was most impressive. It wasn't because of a little bit of luck, but a lot of hard work. My not being in it possibly helped as well. However, the stand out of the whole affair was the costuming, especially the scene at Ascot.

As a matter of interest, I can remember how much we spent to produce this show. In round figures we outlayed $63,000. We received through sponsorships, advertising and ticket sales $72,000.We were running a substantial business, the success of which depended entirely on "bums on seats". We had never applied for government grants and that was a damned good thing. Once you depend on those, you are at the mercy of the bureaucracy and that always ends badly. At this point I will salute all those who put so much time and effort into soliciting advertising in our programs over the years. That money was vital. We were producing such quality performances that advertisers were keen to support us as they knew that we reached a large and discerning audience. One only has to look at the programme for My Fair Lady to see how successful we were in gaining their support. In the very near future it was to be sorely needed.

I was again filled with pride with what we could achieve. We had produced three blockbuster shows in a row. It had taken 20 years but the striving for excellence had paid off. We had a talent pool, both on and off the stage, many a professional company would envy. Quite a few of our young technical bods did go on to work in professional theatre in Melbourne.

Although it was only three years, I regard this as our second golden age.

Another comparison may be to a supernova that flared brilliantly for three years and then collapsed into a black hole.

To be honest though, I was looking forward to finishing my time as President.

# Near Death Experience Resurrection Schism

On arriving back from my trip, there were two situations that caught my attention, one that was expected, one not.

The first, the unexpected one, was that, in my absence, the Committee had been persuaded by the relevant Production Committee to move the Junior show, "Macbeth" from the Little Theatre to the Main Hall. The argument went that as this musical was on the school curriculum this year then lots of students would want to see it and, given the limited capacity of the Little Theatre, we would miss out on the audience. Also by changing the venue,we could employ a much more dramatic lighting and sound plot. Whether the obvious extra costs, which were considerable, were taken into account I do not know. Although I was not there, I can bet that one argument went something like."Without the big hall and all of this extra state-of-art lighting and sound equipment, the show can't possibly be a success in such a limited space as the Little Theatre, etc etc etc..."

I was not happy with this turn of events but, as various contracts had been signed, it was thought too late to reverse it. Even then I should have put my foot down but I didn't. There are a number of reasons for that lack of courage. I was a lame duck as President. I was only going to be there for another two months. What was essentially next years' committee had made this decision, so I figured that it was their baby. The other was that I was mentally spent. I was not up for the inevitable bunfight which would have eventuated, and the deafness in my left ear was not improving and it was starting to affect my right ear as well.

The other situation was to appoint a Production Committee for the

Musical "Follies". That abundance of talent we had now became part of a problem. We had two experienced people apply for the post of Musical Director. We had quite a prolonged discussion at Committee level about the merits of each and it was a difficult decision. I sounded out the Director as to which he thought was the most suitable as he had worked with both in the past. I took his thoughts to the Committee and we opted to go with his choice. I had some misgivings about this as it basically gave the Director the power to appoint the Production Committee in place of the General Committee. I personally approached both applicants to see if a solution could be found to use both of them in the production. Neither would consider being the assistant to the other. When I broke the news to the unsuccessful applicant, it was not received gladly.

That was not a good start to the production. In hindsight, it could be read as an omen.

At the AGM in February I handed over the reins to Lawrie Fildes. I declined to stand for committee as I did not believe past presidents should hang around. A new President should have clear air to work in.

The Junior show, which had by now almost become "as big as Ben Hur" hit the boards.I was told it was a great success artistically, which was all well and good, but financially it was a disaster. It bombed in a big way. The argument that it would attract a large student audience had been wishful thinking. Hardly anyone came. I am ashamed to admit that even I forewent the pleasure. I had no interest in a "Rock Opera". I was no longer on Committee so was under no obligation to go and I was bloody near deaf anyway. The worst aspect of it was that all the extra technical stuff and the move to the hall cost a fortune and to pay for it the reserves built up over the last decade were all but spent, as money from ticket sales was paltry. However hubris and self delusion weren't finished with us yet.

A respite from adversity came with the play "Lend Me a Tenor", an American farce rather than an English one but no less funny for that. Barry Whitehead directed an entertaining cast, mostly of seasoned troupers, but also a couple of newcomers. Most enjoyable, as by now, my deafness was responding to treatment and I could actually hear what was being said on the stage. My right ear was back to normal and the left was improving daily. I believe the show made a modest profit. Thank God, after the disaster of “Macbeth”.

Not being on the Committee meant I was no longer privy to the discussion that occurred at meetings. In modern parlance, I was out of the loop. That did not stop the occasional “leak” coming my way and what I was hearing did not fill me with joy. However, I felt it was not my place to intervene. I was yesterdays’ man.

Originally there was to be a grand staircase as part of the main set. Something that Busby Berkeley would have felt at home with. That and all the sets, as well as lighting and sound equipment, were having to be scaled back dramatically because of a shortage of money. It was fortunate that our credit with the local traders was good. It was to be sorely tested.

In due course the big night came and I went to see “Follies”. I arrived at the theatre and thought that I had the wrong starting time as there were not many people in the foyer. I figured something was amiss as the Front of House people were almost embarrassed to greet me. On entering the hall the reason for their embarrassment became clear: there was almost no one there. There was also no raked seating. I thought: We were back in 1976 at the Morwell Tech. School hall. Like Wagner’s bloody Ring Cycle we’re back where we started 25 years ago. There was no need for ushers. I was invited to take a seat anywhere. The seats were simple stacker chairs. Three hours sitting on one of these is going to give your bum something to think about. I saw a couple of friends and decided to sit with them. As I write this, social distancing has become a watchword. We were 20 years ahead of the game with “Follies”. No trouble at all to provide 2 square metres per patron. We could have had 5 each easily.

Despite all this, I had come to see what Mr. Sondheim could offer, not luxuriate in nicely padded theatre seats. A few years were to pass before that luxury was to befall our “Performing Arts Centre”.

At the appointed time, the music began and we were underway. My friends on stage, and there was quite a crowd of them, were all trying earnestly but making little headway. Interval came and my friends and I looked at each other and asked the same question, "What was all that about?".Even after reading the special insert in the program it made little sense. What was the story? I gathered it was about how a bunch of young mediocraties had developed into a bunch of old has-beens. If the plotline in Frederica was tissue thin then this one made gossamer look like 4-ply. We hoped the cast were enjoying themselves, because the audience wasn't. It must have been disheartening to do your big number to a barely audible outbreak of desultory applause. Anyway, it was interval so time to do something more enjoyable like got to the toilet and then get a few drinks on board to alleviate the pain that was to be Act 2.The atmosphere in the foyer was similar to when tea and curled up sandwiches are had at a dry funeral.{The only thing worse than a dry funeral is a dry wedding.I have had the misfortune to attend both}.

Soon enough the bells are ringing for the start of Act 2. After another quick anaesthetic, and in a funerial frame of mind, my fellow sufferers and I trudged back in to view the corpse one more time. Our expectations were not misplaced. There was to be no half-time resurrection. Another hour or more of bum-numbing, pretentious, overblown, self–centred, incomprehensible theatre was on offer. As it droned on to its long-delayed end I was thinking how thrilling Goethe's love life had been in comparison. In God's good time the end came and we were free at last, dear God, free at last. Polite, pitying applause was given and then we escaped into the night still wondering what the hell it was all about. Earlier in this memoir I described "Frederica "as a dog dropping. "Follies" was an elephants'. My heart went out to the Front of House people who had to watch this night after night.

Back in the 19$^{th}$ century, there was a chap in Italy who the English jokingly called Joe Green[1] who wrote a bit of music for the stage. To ascertain whether he had written a good show, he would hang around the foyer on opening night as the audience left at the end of the show.

1 Actually, his name was Giuseppe Verdi.

If he heard them humming or singing or even whistling any of the tunes from the show, he knew he had a success.

There was no danger of that happening after “Follies”.

I cannot remember one note of any of the music in that show. Not one song has stuck in my memory. I cannot remember any one of the multitude of characters who were on that stage. I did however, learn another of those “Alarm Bells” words. Pastiche.

I had now seen what Mr. Sondheim had to offer. It was a learning experience indeed. Barry Johnston had warned us about doing this show. Unfortunately his was a voice crying in the wilderness. He said that outside of major metropolitan areas, Sondheim was box-office poison. Some things you learn the hard way.

Things did not improve as the season progressed.

The show was a financial disaster. It all but bankrupted the company. Having two huge flops in one year was unprecedented. There were no reserves as “Macbeth” had used most of them up. Ticket sales had to be enough to defray the costs of staging “Follies” even in its severely trimmed down version and having seen the show, there was no way that was going to happen. The crowds stayed away in their thousands. I did wonder at what stage of proceedings did it become obvious to those involved that they were on a theatrical Titanic and the iceberg was bearing down on them.

I think there were a couple of reasons for its flop. The storyline is minimal .I think it’s supposed to be about the characters but there are no characters you really care about, plus there are too many of them, and the music is difficult on the ear. At interval I was almost wishing that I was deaf again. And it went on too long. Its drawbacks were the same as with Frederica, the only difference being that Lehars’ music didn’t set your teeth on edge.

There is a saying that goes....Success has many fathers, failure is an orphan.

The obvious question was: How in the Hell did we manage to be so far up the famous creek with not a paddle in sight? We have not had a digression for some time so let's have one now after I offer you with a few aphorisms....

Do not confuse ability with ambition.

Seldom performed shows are that for a reason.

Do shows that the public wants to see, not shows YOU want them to see.

Bums on seats =money=further shows: No bums on seats =penury=oblivion.

Show selection was ultimately in the hands of the Committee but it would rely to varying degrees, on the advice of the Future Shows sub-committee, henceforth to be known as the FSC. The make- up of this sub- committee was to be of people who had experience in theatre production or who had performed in or directed musical theatre, or taught performing arts at schools or other educational institutions. Their remit was to examine the world of musical theatre to see what would be suitable for the LLOS/LTC. Suitability was determined by a number of factors.

1. Given the venues we have available to us, can we stage the show technically? For example, if we decided to stage Miss Saigon, how do we get a helicopter into our venue?
2. Can we cast the show? Do we have the singers required?
3. Is the music within our capabilities, both vocal and orchestral?
4. Is the show familiar to the public and will it draw an audience to cover the costs of production?
5. Does it target a broad audience? The broader the better as it will have a greater catchment area.

Each of these was to be given equal weight. The FSC had been on the money nearly every time but there were the odd exceptions. The choice of "Macbeth" would have been fine if we had stuck to the original plan but I think the huge successes of the previous three years had gone to their, and subsequently, our heads. We succumbed to the idea that all we had to do was stage a show and the punters would just roll up in numbers to fill a 350 seat venue several times. "Build it and they will come." Bullshit! Refer No 5 above.

The conceit of our invincibility applied equally to "Follies". When it was proposed I had never heard of it along with most of the Committee. However, it came with a strong recommendation from the convenor of the FSC who was a most experienced member of the Company and had directed many shows. His knowledge and experience far outweighed most of ours so we approved his recommendation. The subsequent disaster proved that even the best of us can screw up. Refer No.4 above.

Now back to our situation, which was dire. A Special General Meeting of the Company was called. The whole situation was laid out for the membership and it was grim. If the required finances were not forthcoming then the LTC was finished.

It was decided that approaches would be made to our creditors to negotiate payment plans. Our corporate patron, Loy Yang Power, was a great help by providing their sponsorship money for the next show much earlier than they otherwise would and the City deferred venue rental payments until we were in better shape financially. And lastly, many members dipped into their own pockets to keep the ship afloat with either long term loans or outright donations. We had come full circle again, all the way back to 1963 when the LLOS was first formed. We cobbled together enough to allow us one more go. If this flopped then we really were done for. We could not afford to stage "Wizard of Oz" as planned. Taking our cue from Oliver! we went for a show with lots of kids and "Annie" was the inspired choice. However, there was no possibility of using the Main Hall as the cost of the seating hire was out of the question. Ah well, back to the Little Theatre. We would also do a small non-musical show at the Moe Town Hall. The reason for this was that there were minimal sets and the hall hire was much less that the Little Theatre.

So a very chastened LTC set about restoring its fortunes and reputation. I was almost back on the committee. I was Sponsorship sub-committee chairman. I was the schmoozer in chief. It was vital to keep all the supporters we had garnered over the years despite previous years' disaster and our sub-committee managed to achieve that.

The first production for the year was "Love Letters". This is a play involving two people. They are a couple who have maintained a course of correspondence over a lifetime with all its highs and lows. There is virtually no set. Just two chairs. The actors sit in the chairs and read the correspondence. It doesn't sound much, but if done well it was surprisingly endearing and thought-provoking and Ernie and Christine did it well. We could count that as a success which was good for the morale.

With "Annie" we had the same directors as with Follies except for Choreographer. "Follies" was to be the last show Mandie Black did for the LTC. We were not aware of that at the time. Other events caused this to happen. So thank you Mandie for all your patience, cheerfulness and perseverance. We did, however, have her two daughters, Madeline and Jessica, as orphans as a consolation.

I was encouraged to audition for the part of Drake who is Warbucks' butler. I was given the part. A Minor Principal again! And this involved singing a solo line or two and dancing in an ensemble piece as well as lots of dialogue. No pressure!

Once rehearsals got underway we set to it with a purpose. We wanted to replicate Oliver,or Fiddler, not Follies.There were two sets of kids so two sets of ancillary bums to put on seats. The casting was right on if I say so myself. I had no trouble being the dignified English butler. After all, I was an honours graduate of the Iolanthe School of Pompous Poncing! Remembering lines and dance steps was another thing altogether.

Oliver! had brought us a talented crew of kids such as Amy and Chris Larsen, Ashley Vanyai, Nick Kong and Ben Jenner. Annie was to be even more fruitful. Casey Hall, Jessie Waugh, Rebecca Lay, Jaz. Flowers, Laura Hartnell to name just a few. Just as with Oliver!, having all those talented youngsters around put a bounce into everyone's step. Another benefit of doing a show with kids is that, strangely enough, they have parents and they may also want to become involved. Such was the case with Casey Hall's dad, John. When it came to set design and construction he was to prove himself a genius.

We were going to show that “Follies” had been an aberration.

As the season approached, we knew we had a show. Ticket sales were going well. All those kids would be spreading the word. Publicity posters and fliers were all over the Valley. Everything was going swimmingly until the first dress rehearsal when Warbucks' household maids made their entrance. Their French Maids costumes caused a stir in the prude section of the FC.”This is a childrens' show” was the cry.”The hems on those skirts must come down!” they added. It was duly done. Pity, a couple of those girls had nice sets of pins. Just as well there were no Grisettes in this show. And so opening night was upon us.

The Show was a huge success. The LTC was back in business. I had a great time. I only goofed up four times for the season. These things did not happen early in the piece. I was concentrating too hard at that time for anything to go wrong. After a few performances I started to relax, thinking I had it down pat. Oh, you foolish, foolish boy! Occasion one...In the scene where the Warbucks household do their opening song and dance Drake sings two lines. I had done this without problems many times in rehearsal and in the early performances. One night something distracted me and I dried when I was to sing my bit. I totally lost what I was to sing. I uttered some gibberish and the whole thing just kept on going as normal. I have no idea what the audience made of what happened. I did, however, see a vey quizzical look on Ernie's face as he was conducting. He did inquire at interval as to what happened. I told him I had dried and he said that if anyone asks, say it was a fault with the lapel mike, but try not to do it again. That was very forgiving of him. It never happened again but from then on he was always glaring up at me mouthing the words when I was about to sing my bit. On the plus side, I never once cocked up the dance steps. If the dance routine in Fiddler was my Everest,then Annie was my K2. Occasion two....At the end of that scene, Warbucks' secretary Miss Farrell makes her entrance and is greeted by Drake, addressing her by name. One night, on she comes and yours truly says, ”Good morning Miss Hannigan.” WRONG! Miss

Hannigan is the villain who runs the orphanage and the audience has met her in the previous scenes. The moment I said it I knew I had goofed and very quickly came back with "Miss Farrell". But in live theatre words can't be unsaid. I copped a bit of flak about that one, especially from Christine. I promised to be good and try not to do it again. Occasion three...When not on the Theatre stage we loitered around the stage of the adjacent Town Hall. It was some distance from the stage of the Little Theatre with various small props and back stage crew in between. On this occasion I was merrily chatting away and not paying attention to the action in the theatre until I heard my cue being uttered rather loudly. With speed that would have made Superman jealous, I made towards my entrance, pulling up just out of sight, so I could enter with my dignity intact. I was, however, too out of breath to say my lines for quite a few seconds. It had been some years since being admonished but there was no avoiding it this time. Occasion 4....I think it was in the Hooverville scene that I had to say a line an offstage. It was "Hey Man! Keep it quiet down there!" with the appropriate accent. I was told later that it sounded more Jamaica than New York. Near enough. It had to be delivered from up on the scenery scaffolding .To get there required climbing up a ladder and stepping onto a wooden platform. One night when performing this feat of mountaineering, I hit my shin on one of the brackets holding the scaffolding together. An expletive was uttered and apparently heard quite clearly in the wings and probably on the stage. Fortunate there was a bit of action happening on the stage at the time so hopefully it wasn't heard in the audience.

Everyone in live theatre knows that small props are your enemy. As an English butler, a bowler hat was part of my costume. For one scene I had to make an entrance, remove my hat and hang it on the hall stand. The peg on the hall stand was straight. It should have been made with a slight uptilt of the peg. Bowler hats are firm. And round. If they are not placed firmly onto the peg they may fall off. It did. A clever save by one of the now demurely dressed maids stopped the thing from rolling around the stage. The appropriate alteration was made to the peg. Towards the end of the show there is the scene when a proposed Xmas party is cut short when the Mudges turn up. Drake has to turn the Xmas lights off and exit stage. Do you think those bloody lights would switch off every time? No. My switch was not the actual one that did the deed. They weren't silly enough to trust me with that. Someone else had that task. It was a challenge to think up enough ad-libbing as the fault was fixed and even then the lights went off when I was just standing there nowhere near the switch.

Over the years I've tried not to boast about my achievements on the stage, most likely because there have been so very few of them, but in Annie I had my big moment. Towards the end of act 2 there is scene when it seems Annie will be adopted by Warbucks. Drake, the stuffy old English butler has taken a shine to Annie and so is delighted with that prospect but keeps his emotions well in check when others are around. Drake is the last to exit the stage in this scene. The book says he is to jump and click his heels together with joy as he exits. Try as I might I could not achieve this feat without nearly falling arse over head every time. I was as ungainly as a new-born foal. I suggested to David Pickburn that seeing I was hopeless at that move, how about I do a scissor kick which, to the amazement of all, I could do easily. [ There was more to me than just being a pompous poncer !] So every performance, Drake would stride half- way across the stage in dignified fashion then, without breaking stride, do the scissor kick, land in step, and continue off stage as if the kick never happened. Exit applause every time! David said exit applause is the Holy Grail of everyone in live theatre. A bloke could get a swelled head if he was not careful. He might then behave like a Minor Principal. Of course, it never entered my head that something might go wrong so I got a real surprise when doing this choreographic masterpiece one night I landed slightly off-centre and ricked my knee. I could hear the theatre Gods saying "Do your scissor kick now, bighead! " I did manage but it was not as high and it hurt each time. More suffering for the sake of art.

Looking back to that show there were some terrific performances.

Lawrie as Warbucks was another of his great characterisations. I had not previously been in a show with Beth Millar but I was knocked out by her performance as Miss Hannigan. She really came across as a nasty, mean old bitch which was totally the opposite to her in real life. Both Mikaela and Casey as our two Annies were great, plus the two of them were such pleasant and polite youngsters and Laura Hartnell as Molly stole the hearts of the audience every time. All the kids were great. And lastly, Barry Whitehead as Roosevelt was uncanny. You almost felt he had just stepped out of an old newsreel.

You bet! The LTC was definitely back in business. We were going to do another great show next year, "The King and I". Well known by the public, great characters, great music and libretto, lots of kids. It had it all .So what could possibly go wrong? It wasn't long in coming.

The AGM came in February at which it was announced that Jenny Johnston and Jan Pickburn were our new Life Members. Both were richly deserved as both had given great service to the LLOS and the LTC in many capacities over many years.

The other great news was that we had made a good profit from Annie and so we were able to clear our debts and have enough to seed the new show. Applicants had been called for the Production Committee and those successful were to be announced shortly after the AGM. There had been several applicants for the position of Director.

The announcement that Barry Whitehead had been given the nod was the catalyst for the third and most painful unpleasantness. To everyone's great surprise, David Pickburn took it badly and personally, yet he was railing against the very system he had been so assiduous in putting into place. Just as the directing team had the right to choose the cast, it was the prerogative of the Committee to appoint the directorial team, and had always been the case. Over ten years previous to this event, David had insisted that all directors have assistants so as to train up new people for when the time came and we had embarked on the course of doing multiple shows each year with this also in mind. It had now come to pass that we had several people who could direct shows quite successfully. I only got embroiled in this when I received a letter from David stating his case and asking for support. Many other members also were canvassed. I read it many, many times and could not believe it had come from a fellow I had known and regarded as a close friend for over 25 years. To be forced to take sides was truly horrible. I felt that I could not support his proposition that he should be allowed to keep the directors role until he decided to retire from it. Not even Prime Ministers get that opportunity. I fell severely out of favour. It was a desperately sad, sad time as David and Jan departed and a number of others went with him [ as well did a part of my soul.] And sadly, he left behind quite a few others hurt and bewildered.

With a gloom having descended onto the LTC, we auditioned for the show. There were only two very minor roles for me to go for, The ship's Captain and the British Ambassador. I got neither. The ship's captain is supposed to be Scottish so I assumed that my Sco'ish arksent was nae gude enough but I thought my Drake- like dignity would get the other part. Not so. Maybe next year. Maybe I could actually spend a bit more time in my dental practice. I couldn't wait to see the show though.

# BACK IN BUSINESS
# A THIRD GOLDEN AGE

Despite the gloomy atmosphere left by the great unpleasantness, the company put it behind it and concentrated on making the "King and I" a success.[and without me no less!] I was very much out of the loop now. I did feel a little lost, given the intensity of my involvement over the last eight years and too many of those I had counted as friends had gone due to the unpleasantness. Consequently there was not much I can say about what happened that year except that, due to the recent turbulence, we would be doing only one show this year.

In due course, the season came around and to the show I went. It was terrific. Lawrie gave another great characterisation as the King although when it came to the dying scene, I reckoned he had read Michael Green [Remember him from an earlier chapter?] a bit too closely. All the kids were great. Talk about scene stealers. Quite a few had made the transition from orphans one year to royal children the next without blinking an eye. To my mind though, Simon Hemming as the Kralahome, was the pick of the performers [with or without moccasins]. This was his break-out show.

I was jealous as all hell. Being on the Sponsorship sub-committee was good but did not compare with being on the stage. I wanted back in.

Next years' show was to be "$42^{nd}$ St". When I looked at the requirements re choreography I figured that maybe this was not the show for me. I decided to go on a well- deserved holiday instead. Of course I went to see the show. I was right about the choreography. Way out of my league. I did get one hell of a shock when I entered the theatre. The old orange buckets were gone and had been replaced by real theatre seats !!! Ones with upholstered seats that could be raised and lowered, ones with padded arm rests, you know, the ones that every other theatre in the country had had since JC played full back for Jerusalem. And to add to this miraculous state of affairs, the Council had renovated the Main Hall area and had installed retractable raked seating. Maybe it finally dawned on them that their Performing Arts Centre was really no such thing. Naturally, the concept of a real built-for-purpose facility was still just a dream.

As I had not been part of it, I did not know the show in detail but it all seemed to go off well and was well received by the audience. The night I attended it was in the middle of the season and there was a good house, so I assumed that it made a profit. Apart from Brooke Soutar as the lead, I don't recall any particular performances standing out but that's more a comment on my memory than anything else. One thing I do clearly remember is an avalanche of tap dancers filling the stage. It also announced the arrival of another future star in Daniel Hanson. Small in stature, large in talent and generous in character.

As I mentioned earlier, I decided to visit central Europe on my way to the FDI congress in Vienna. The memories of "Fiddler" and its impact on me were still fresh in my mind, so to visit the various sites around Krakow associated with the Holocaust was quite confronting as was a visit to the Old Jewish quarter in Prague. There was also a very good little Jewish museum in Bratislava where I was shocked to be told it still gets vandalised with swastikas on a regular basis. Another part of my trip was a visit to Istanbul which I loved and then Gallipoli which was another onslaught on my emotions. I had a stopover in Singapore on the way home. The night I arrived there was the night of the Bali bombings. I awoke that Sunday morning not knowing what had happened until I put the TV on. As I sat transfixed by what I was seeing, it dawned on me that the evil that had brought about Auschwitz was still very much with us. Never before have I been so happy to step out of the plane at Tullamarine.

The year 2002 had also brought the glad tidings that Kate Dougan,

Max and Ann Maloney were all honoured with Life Memberships of the LTC. Each and every one very much deserved.

Maybe my chance to tread the boards again might come in 2003. We were doing "Hello Dolly" and we were going back to the Main Hall as it now had raked seating installed by our dear Council, which meant we did not have to hire it as we had done for "Oliver!", "Fiddler", or "My Fair Lady". We could now afford to use the Main Hall. I duly auditioned for the part of the Judge and got it. I was back up there one more time. Whoopee!! The Judge is a small part at the end of the show so I had the pleasure of watching virtually the whole show every night before I was required. I did not get bored once. There was a vitality and sparkle about the whole show. It would be hard to pick one performer over any other. Christine Skicko as Dolly was in her flamboyant element. Newcomer Mark Woods was bang-on as Vandergelder, Brooke and Casey as Irene and Minnie Faye also. But the most memorable and hilariously funny were Nick Kong and Dan Clancey as Barnaby and Cornelius. The MC with their Waiters' Gallop was a revelation! At the end of the whole business I got to do my bit. My whole stage time was about 15 minutes. Remembering the lesson from "Pinafore" twenty years previously, that it is very difficult to overact in live theatre, I gave it every shot in the arsenal, including ad-libs. More ham than Coles' Deli!

The scene opens with all the main characters crowded into the dock, charged with a whole raft of offences and loudly bickering amongst themselves. The Judge [me] is calling for quiet and is being ignored until he raises his voice to a shout on his third attempt and bangs his gavel firmly. One rehearsal all was going to plan except the mob didn't shut up so I called out a 4$^{th}$ time "Quiet, Goddammit!" Brooke looked at me and then to Barry, saying that wasn't in the script. Barry seemed to have liked it so in it went. As had been the case over all those years, I couldn't leave well enough alone. I added the odd word on a couple of occasions and got away with it until brought into line by the Director. It was the banging of the gavel that brought admonishment. As the season progressed I was really getting into it until the gavel hit the wooden block a bit too hard. The head of the gavel flew off into the mob in the dock and the wooden block split in half, with the two pieces scudding across the stage like two hockey pucks. The audience all thought it was part of the show and laughed accordingly. My courtroom assistant, Craigen Whitehead had a ringside seat to my shenanigans and I could hear him sniggering some nights. He says he learnt an awful lot from me watching those performances. In what respect he didn't say. I had had fifteen minutes on the stage hamming it up to the max and guess what? I received a commendation from the Musical Theatre Guild of Victoria! They must have been easily impressed.

We had a cracker of a show. Great performances all round .We certainly were back in business with a bang and it was great to be part of it again. This show heralded the arrival of another long term stalwart by name of Kara Smith.

Having mentioned the Music Theatre Guild of Victoria, I might go on another diversion to explain their relevance.

The MTGV was set up in Melbourne in 1986 by a group of people who had been active in amateur musical theatre for many years with the aim of providing a forum for people of like mind to meet and to share their knowledge and experience. All amateur groups in Victoria were encouraged to affiliate, which the LLOS duly did. Each year they had an awards night for achievements in a wide range of categories, although Best Production was the one everyone coveted the most because it encompassed everyone who had been part of it from cast to crew to all the back stage people in lighting, costumes, millinery, hairstylist, make up, everything, although any award was gratefully received. In fact, to even be nominated for an award was a feather in one's cap. Below that standard were Commendations, again gratefully received. There were upward of seventy companies throughout the state affiliated with the MTGV, so the competition was quite stiff and hence to win an award was a notable achievement. To be in consideration of an award the company invited the MTGV to provide three judges to see our show and give critiques. We never knew when the judges would attend. The fact that we did not know the judges and they would not have much knowledge of us gave their opinions credibility and objectivity. Also the fact that these people had long experience in not just amateur theatre but also semi-professional and even professional theatre gave re-assurance that they knew what they were talking about.

Now, within this diversion, we will now have a digression.

Theatre companies can be roughly divided between three groups of people. Firstly, there are the Theatricals aka the Artistes and then there is the Rest, with a small group of special people who straddle both camps. We shall call them the Straddlers. They are rare and need to be treasured and any tendency to fall into the camp of the Artistes has to be thwarted. They are the ones who need to have their heads in the clouds but their feet on the ground. They realise that artistic vision comes with a price tag so it all revolves around money i.e. bums on seats. The Artistes have the visions of how a show will look, how the lighting plot will unfold, how a character will be portrayed, how stunning the choreography will be, how breathtaking the sets will be and how all this will enhance their performance, irrespective of the size of the audience. The Rest join up to have the experience of being on the stage where they can have a go as a character if they pass the audition but if not, they can be in the chorus to enjoy singing and to also enjoy the camaraderie, as well as displaying what talent they may have to their family and friends. They certainly don't do it for Awards as for most such a thing is not on their radar. They know instinctively that shows are put on for the benefit of the audience, not the performers. They also trust the Future Shows sub-committee to choose wisely.

The role of the Straddlers to entice the Rest to sign up to the vision of the Artistes and convince them that the chosen show will appeal to a wide audience and you will have a memorable and happy experience. When that merger is successful, you get a great show. We have seen what happens when it doesn't.

Enough digression, back to the diversion.

Not long after the creation of the MTGV, those who ran the local performing arts companies, came together to set up a Gippsland version, called the Gippsland Amateur Theatre Awards, GAT for short. This was in the halcyon days of the late 1980s when there were many more companies in existence. There were to be two divisions, Musical and Non-Musical. Before I went onto the Committee I was aware of such an organisation but didn't really pay much attention to it. Receiving an award for doing my bit wasn't ever going to happen so I thought, Good Luck to those who might. It was only when I became President I needed to look more seriously at it. In 1995 I was actually invited to present one of the awards at the Awards Presentation night in the theatre in Warragul. I was there in an official capacity as we were in the running for a best production award which we duly won with "Charlie Girl". This was the first time I had met the worthies of the GAT. After the presentations there was a "champagne" supper where all the members of the component companies mingled, enthusiastically air-kissing cheeks and all saying how wonderful everyone was but you got the feeling that the claws were only retracted so far as to be not noticeable. Most of my conversations were short as they tended to fizzle out when my fellow conversant realised that I was not one "Them". I was not a Theatrical. I had not been to Teacher's College to study Drama and Performance. Nor had I been to University to do an Arts Degree. I had wasted my time there doing dentistry. When that piece of information entered the conversation, the reaction was as if I had farted in a lift. People seemed to take a step backwards. [Not that I would ever do such a thing! Well, not since my student days]. The concept that a dentist having a yen for Musical Theatre seemed to be beyond grasping. No doubt about it, I was most certainly one of the Rest. I have since had a rather jaundiced view of GAT. Whilst President I attended the Presentation Nights as a duty, pleased when one of our lot won an award but not doing handstands about it. I suppose it kept the Artistes in the company happy. There were also the occasional "John MacEnroe" moments when some winners were announced, i.e."You can't be serious" being hissed through clenched teeth somewhere behind me.

The main reason I had little regard for GAT was that, as President, I was privy to the critiques of the shows by both GAT and MTGV. The latter were written by people who knew what they were talking about. The former were written by people who thought they knew what they were talking about.

I was never reluctant to have our efforts judged by our peers. However, in time I came to regard GAT judges as neither objective nor credible. Some of their critiques were fanciful or petty to the extreme and some were just malicious put downs. I did not regard them as our peers. The fundamental problem was that the judging panel was too small and were well known to most of the performers. There was no chance of anonymity and personal prejudices could not be discounted. I can recall being in the dressing room being costumed and made-up when one of the front-of –house people would come down and announce that the GAT judges were in the audience. A little quiver of excitement would run through the room. The more minor the principal, the more pronounced the quiver. Personally, I couldn't have given a stuff. I regarded the whole thing as just irrelevant to most of us. When I heard that we had left GAT, I just thought ....no great loss. I doubt if being part of it ever sold one extra ticket.

The year 2004 was approaching and to show we were really on a roll we were going to do two shows once again.

As good as that was, there occurred a real game-changer for the company. We had secured from the Council a premises to call our own; somewhere to rehearse, somewhere to store costumes away from the Hut, somewhere to have our meetings. In short, Home. It was to become "The Wings". In his five years as President, this, I think, was Lawrie's crowning achievement.

Our first show for the year was to be "West Side Story". Lawrie was to be Director. Clutching my MTGV commendation tightly to my bosom, I auditioned for the role of Doc and was successful. We still had to rehearse at the Hexagon at the University as we could not take up residence at the Wings until later in the year.

Recalling how hard it had been to get a male chorus in our earlier years, I was pleasantly surprised to see how many men auditioned to be members of the gangs. This involved quite a bit of complex choreography. Times had certainly changed. As it turned out, these boys would have found the cachuca a doddle. The WUBWT principle had very definitely been made redundant.

"West Side Story" is one of those iconic shows that every company worth its salt wants to do. Being able to do shows such as this was the main driving force behind the transition from LLOS to LTC.

This production also brought in an innovation in the rehearsal schedule. Just before going into the theatre we were to have a rehearsal camp at a local school camp called Woorabinda for a weekend of solid work to really polish our performance and to further enhance the camaraderie of the company. This was to become a regular part of the rehearsal schedule for as long as I was active in the company because it fulfilled its aims admirably.

There was plenty of hard work done but we had a great cast and even early on we knew we had a show. The final rehearsals at Judy Gray's Dance Studio had us bursting to get into the theatre. It was there that Lawrie tackled the delicate issue of the assault scene in Doc's drug store involving Anita and the Jets. How realistic can you make it? Jaz Flowers who played Anita had the final say. She was pretty brave in her decision and it was always her call.

When we did bump into the theatre what a sight beheld us.

I mentioned John Hall earlier. The set he designed and built was gobsmacking. Even after the so-called upgrade of the so-called "Performing Arts Centre" there was still limited wing space and no fly space, so scenery and sets had to be designed with these limitations in mind. John had the ability to see a space and think in three dimensions so that sets rotated, spiralled, and even unfolded, scenery was on castors and was double faced. Changing scenes every night was a cross between a ballet and constructing a 3-D jigsaw as each piece was put in place and the next piece locked into it. Hats off to the crew who did this with such speed and precision. It was a show in itself!

The casting was spot on as well. The two leads, Nick Kong and Jessie Waugh were just wonderful and perfect for their roles in ability and age. The whole ensemble was great. The supporting roles were also strong. Simon Hemming as Bernardo was quite menacing and Jaz Flowers as Anita was a star. The dancing was spectacular. What a far cry from days past. Mandie Black had certainly laid some solid foundations but the choreographers who had emerged since then had taken the company to a stunning height of excellence. Lynne Vanderzalm, Judy Gray, Penny-Lee and Bridie Tompkins, Brooke Soutar,and their other assistants please take a bow! There were a few minor roles such as Doc { the only old bloke in it, me], Lieut.Schrank, Bernard Dettering in his first outing with the LTC and Officer Krupke, Gary Wellsmore playing an American cop this time. His last outing was a Russian heavy in "Fiddler".

The stand out performer was Jessie Waugh. Perfect in her role and heartbreaking in her performance. An absolute joy to watch her, Nick and Jaz every time and a real privilege to share a stage with them.

I was delighted to get the part of Doc. No singing and no dancing! Another jackpot! However this time I had to actually ACT, instead of hamming it up to rafters like last time. At the very first rehearsal, Lawrie sat with us bit players and went through our parts as he saw them and then asked each of us to do the same with each others' roles. He stressed that he saw these minor roles as integral to the story, not superfluous extras. I'd never been through this procedure before. Was this what real actors did ? With this in mind, into rehearsal we went and I really tried to become the world weary old bloke who was Doc. I was in a couple of scenes in Act 1 and then in the penultimate two scenes where it all comes to a head and Doc totally loses it. When it came to the real performances, I was "in the zone". When the assault scene occurs in my Drug Store, I come up onto the stage in a fury and start roughing up the gang members. Several times the boys said afterwards to turn it down a bit as I was ripping their clothes and if my nails were a tiny bit long, leaving vivid scratches. At one point after I have chucked them out, I thought of picking up a chair and throwing it after them but Lawrie thought flying chairs were a bit of a hazard so that bit of business did not eventuate. I had the stage to myself. It was dead silence. I could hear the audience holding their breath. I was trying to get mine back. I then go down to the cellar where I have a confrontation with Tony, during which I am to slap him across the face. Most times I did it properly and missed. A couple of times I connected. All this was going on about three metres from the front row of the audience. The first time I connected it made quite a sound. Nick had a really startled look on his face as head swung towards the audience who, having heard the slap and thinking it was part of the proceedings, let out quite a gasp. Nick to his great credit did not miss a beat. I did apologise profusely after the show and he was quite forgiving. When it happened the second time he wasn't quite so forgiving afterwards as I had promised to be good and not do it again. It is a wrenching scene and after it finishes I am again alone, this time on the floor of the hall, a broken man. All through this scene I could hear the sobbing in the audience as the tragic end of the show is played out. As I made my silent way up the stairs I was often in tears myself. Was this what happens to real actors? It was that quiet you could have heard a mouse hiccup.

I was to be on the stage for most of 33 years .That part was the best thing I ever did on stage. The MTGV must have thought it wasn't too shabby as they gave me another Commendation. This time I felt that I had actually earned it. Bernard Dettering got one as well. He was to have quite an impact on the company over the years. There has to be some small irony in that I received two Commendations from the MUSIC Theatre Guild of Victoria for performances that involved absolutely no singing or dancing.

The show was a huge success as well it should have been. For what it's worth, I put it as the second best show we ever did. To my mind, nothing would surpass " Fiddler", 1997 version. Towards the end of the season the cast and crew were all called to the Little Theatre for an important announcement. Wondering what was afoot, we all went and sat down in anticipation. Our new President Keiri Byers announced that Lawrie Fildes was our latest Life Member. Well done Lawrie. Much appreciative applause. For once in his life Lawrie was lost for words.

Having packed away "West Side Story", we were next to produce "Stepping Out", a play with choreography. I wisely resisted the temptation to audition. The level of competence in the choreography required had risen steeply over the last few years and mine had not. As well, I was now into my mid-fifties so any youthful suppleness had long since vanished. If there was a part with minimal or no singing or dancing, I was your man.

This show was to be the first to be rehearsed in our new home.

The production went well, although the subject matter was a bit more serious than other plays had been.

Just before "Stepping Out" was to be staged, the LTC lost one of its Life Members in Harry Dougan after a short illness. Harry was a foundation member of the LLOS and had performed in many roles both in the early days of the LLOS and again later with the LTC. He retired from the stage after the 1994 Merry Widow but in his later years he was our program seller par excellence. Only at his funeral did I learn that he had been a fellow Melbourne supporter all these years. That helped to explain why he was always such a true gentleman.

By now, I had ceased my involvement with the sponsorship sub-committee. I did take on the role of Public Officer after my old Apex mate Bob Lyall had relinquished the position. Despite its title, it was not an onerous position. Later in the year, I was invited to join the Committee for the annual committee dinner ostensibly because of my role as PO. It was an excuse. When I arrived, rather puzzled that the position of PO had assumed such importance, I was greeted with the announcement that I was now a Life Member of the LTC. My turn to be lost for words.

The year 2005 was approaching and we were to do two shows again. Having achieved such a result with "West Side Story" we again aimed high. Our big production was to be "Cabaret".

Having actually made an impact with Doc, I was being urged to audition for Herr Schultz and I certainly gave the idea some thought but my heart wasn't in it as I was experiencing hearing problems again. Mark Woods did it far better than I would ever have done. However, I was back in the chorus. This is another of our shows that is right up there with our best. It has a strong storyline with strong characters, memorable music that the public knew and it had a terrific cast. As well as the Principals, everyone else had a persona, especially in the scenes in the Kit Kat Club. I was an old roué cosying up to one of the fellows who played the part of a cross-dresser. Later I was a sailor who was a customer of Fraulein Kost and then a waiter and then in the "Money Money" scene. Some rapid costume changes were needed.

This was the first major show we rehearsed at the "The Wings". What a difference having such space made, as well as having separate rooms to rehearse different bits simultaneously.

So with our usual enthusiasm we launched into our rehearsal. At the first one we sat and analysed our characters, and everyone else's. And then it was "Wilkommen, Bienvenue, Welcome..." and away we went.

It wasn't long before we knew our show was going to be a cracker. Getting into character took a bit of learning as I hadn't had much practice in cosying up to well-muscled transvestites up until then. Then again, it probably was a first for the fellow who played that role as well. I was quite relieved to know that snogging was not required. I can only assume those members of the FC who had been cast as hookers were facing a similar challenge.

However, my biggest challenge was in the Money,Money song as I had to lead the men's chorus onto the stage AT THE RIGHT CUE! The gods of choreography were taunting me.

As rehearsal gathered pace, I became aware that I was seeing some great performances developing .I could hardly wait to see what it would be like on the stage.

As we had done the previous year we, had the rehearsal camp at Woorabinda. I can recall sitting around the camp fire after we had finished on the Saturday night having some well–earned drinks .I was not in this discussion but I could hear a deep and meaningful discourse from one of the Directing team about totemic spirituality amongst native American peoples and how we also could have such a thing. Really? At this point, one of the group of mostly young females being regaled with this, asked what his totem was and, of course, it was an eagle. What else could it have been? A frog or skink or a stink bug would never do. I turned away to resume my conversation with another couple of the MC with the phrase "New Age Psychobabble" in my mind. We were discussing football and the merits of various alcoholic beverages. We were definitely part of the Rest. Artistes like to have totems. The Rest like a drink.

When that time came John Hall and his team had again come up with a masterpiece. The lighting guru had also procured a thing called a Gobo. Then to top it off we had a revolving stage![which lasted the whole season before breaking down on the final night]. Broadway, eat your heart out!

As expected the show was a hit. I can remember the opening number as if it was yesterday. We were in the Kit Kat Club with the Kit Kat girls draped over their chairs in languid but alluring fashion with the spotlights focused tightly on them. From where I was sitting and where the spot was aiming, I had great difficulty remembering to sing. I'm sorry Grisettes of 1976, and Charlie Girls' Girls; although this was only the opening number, you have already been surpassed.

When I look back on the individual performances each and everyone was top notch, but one stands out. In all the years I have been watching or participating in the LLOS/LTC productions, I regard the performance of Brice Sedgwick as the Emcee as the best individual performance I ever saw in any show. It was riveting, night after night.

Not far behind him was Kara Smith as Sally Bowles. A brilliant performance. Brash, sexy, fragile. Simon Hemming as Cliff was great because Cliff is a bit of a wimp and it needs effort to make him interesting and Simon was able to do that.

There were many memorable scenes. Everything with Brice in it was memorable but his dancing in the kickline at the start of Act 2 was especially so and the poignancy of the Gorilla song brought a tear to the eye. Above all, his leering lechery as the Emcee was mesmerising.

Annette O'Shea had made her debut with "Stepping Out" the previous year. In this show she put in a stirling performance as Fraulein Kost, the sailors' "friend". There is not a lot of humour in this show but there is a bit in act 1 and I was part of it as one of three sailors who had been entertained by Frau Kost in her room. We exit one after the other from her room into the living room of Fraulein Schneider's house. Barry Whitehead, the director, showed a sense of humour in casting the three sailors. First to emerge from Fraulien Kosts' room was Daniel Hanson who is rather short and slight of build, then Andrew Braniff of medium height and build, and lastly me, who is slightly taller than Andrew and certainly of heavier build. At this point there is no written dialogue for us. The audience had gotten the joke and were having a bit of a giggle as we did our exits. However, I thought it was a bit flat. I reckoned that after having had our jollies with Fraulein Kost we would have been in a fairly chirpy frame of mind. So I added some ad libs and was not admonished by Barry. In fact, he tacitly encouraged it. Firstly it was as I handed the money to Annette, I said "Danke, oh danke,mien liebchen". I had not advised Annette I was going to do it, so when I said it there was a "where did that come from" sort of look on her face, but she quickly twigged and got into spirit of things. Some wag said we were trying to write a whole new scene into the show. Another time as I was exiting I called "Oh, wunderbar," and later in the season I came out with "What a woman!" with appropriate Germanic accent. The backstage crew were having a good laugh each night and were wondering what I was going to say next. At this point Barry suggested that we curb ourselves and leave things as they were, as the other two sailors were starting to get ideas. After one show, I was mingling with friends in the foyer and one of them was German and she complimented me on my accent when I said bits in German! Unfortunately she was not from the MTGV.

In between scenes, there were some rapid costume changes needed.

Getting into the waiters outfit for their song "Tomorrow belongs to me" wasn't too bad, but there was precious little time to get into the shiny silver suit for "Money,Money" .It was chaos in the wings and on the Little Theatre stage as we got our costumes on. There was no time to go down to the dressing rooms. We were assisted by a team of dressers who had our costumes all ready as we exited from the stage in the Hall. Ladies, and my dresser Jan Smith in particular, I don't doubt you saw some sights you had never seen before and probably wouldn't care to again, so your discretion has to be acknowledged and appreciated. As mentioned earlier, I was to lead the MC onto the stage in a sort of swaggering gait. It was crucial that it happen at a particular point. I thought I had beaten the stage fright thing years ago but it had now decided to make a come-back. It was not helped by members of the MC behind me saying " now " when even I knew it was the wrong moment. Bastards! These blokes were no better than those 30 years before them. Anyway, we managed to do the scene without cocking it up too badly and then it was another lightning costume change into the sailors rig.

The waiters scene introduced the "Fatherland " song which caused a real raising of the hairs on the neck. You could feel the menace then but when it was sung at the end of Act 1 to ruin the party in the fruit shop it was chilling because the Gobo had projected a giant swastika onto the cyclorama behind us. I was told by audience members that they felt personally frightened and intimidated by it.

Act 1 sets the stage for the tragedy, act 2 plays it out. There is no more humour. The shadow of the swastika dominates the story. You know that all these people are doomed and nothing they do can prevent it. The impact of Kara's rendition of "Cabaret" was electric. When the Nazi thugs arrive and bust up the place, you just want out. Even today, the memory of those swastika armbands sends a shudder down my spine. Remember, I had been to Auschwitz not that long before this.

Apart from its wonderful music, 'Cabaret" works because it has such a strong story and it has people that you care about.

You care about Sally Bowles and you desperately wish she would take the chance to leave with Cliff, but you know deep down she can't. You care about Herr Schultz who is doomed by his birth and Fraulein Schneider who will be doomed by her marriage. You care about the Emcee who is equally doomed by what he is, not who he is or what he does. You care about all the inhabitants of the demi-monde who, despite the sleaze and debauchery of their world, they have a higher level of morality than the Nazis who destroy them.

This show was on a par with "West Side Story" for impact and quality of performance. One last note needs to be made about the programs for the recent shows. They had become quite erudite treatises on the times and places in which our shows were set. I learnt more about interwar Berlin than ever I had known beforehand or possibly ever needed to know.

After two gruelling and emotionally exhausting shows, next year we were going to do a show with a happy ending. Get your colour swatches out, it's "Joseph and the Technicolour Dreamcoat" coming to a theatre near you.

Meanwhile we were going to do a one act play in Foster for the FAMDA festival of one act plays. It was called "Cracking the Whip" and it had a cast of five who I'm told enjoyed themselves.

I did not see it. I had difficulty recalling anything about it. I'm glad I didn't see it as the main character is a neurotic dentist.

Speaking of neurotic dentists, I had decided to take a long break almost straight after "Cabaret" had finished. I was planning to spend seven weeks in Canada as the FDI Congress was in Montreal that year. I had been planning the trip since January and had been seeking a locum since then. I was going to visit most of the country, Nunavut, Yukon, NW Territories, and more. I was going to visit friends in Winnipeg and Vancouver. Even while the show was in production I was still trying to get a locum. I was unsuccessful in that regard and had to cancel the whole trip 48 hrs before I was due to fly out. To say that I was extremely pissed off with the world would be a massive understatement! I was in no state mentally just to shrug my shoulders and mutter too bad. I told my staff what had transpired and I would see them in two weeks when they could start booking patients again. At this time I was on my own in the practice and could not afford to take seven weeks off. I had spent 25 years building the practice. Seven weeks away would have seen it vanish.

I decided to head to East Gippsland for a while to sort my mind out. It was August so it was out of season and not during school holidays so getting accommodation was not difficult or expensive. I left Morwell on the Monday afternoon to stay a couple of nights at Metung. Somehow I resisted the temptation to get totally plastered that night. The next day I went to Lakes Entrance for a round of golf. I was still in the foulest of moods, a situation not improved by my hitting my first three shots into the lake next to the first hole. As the round progressed the golf did not improve and the weather was starting to match my mood. That night the blizzard struck. It snowed throughout the whole of Gippsland. The rain back in Metung was frozen and horizontal. As I huddled next to the fire after having dinner at the pub, I did the sums on how much I could make as a locum as against owning a practice. That was my 'light bulb moment". I realised a man was a bloody fool to be doing what I was doing as regards practicing dentistry. When I returned to Morwell, the first thing I told my staff was that the practice was on the market. Getting a buyer was the challenge. It would take two years before a potential buyer made a realistic offer. I thought I had a buyer in December of 2005 but that fell through but I thought.... maybe in the New Year?

Delighted as I was that "Joseph" was to be our major show, I was surprised to say the least that we were going to do "Into the Woods" as a second and supposedly minor production. Sondheim? Again? Some people have exceedingly short memories. Did we not learn anything from the folly of "Follies"? My attitude to us having anything to do with a Sondheim show was made very clear in a previous chapter. I heard the usual stuff about how wonderful the music was and characters are really interesting etc.etc. and it's a great show to be in. My reply was."That may be so. Let's see how many turn up to see it." Out of a sense of duty, I was one of them. One pleasing aspect that was a relief, was that the sets were not on the "De Mille " scale and hence had not cost a fortune as was the case with "Follies". Nevertheless the result was the same. Bugger all audience meant it made a loss. How unexpected! The same audience that stayed away from "Follies" in their thousands did so again and why wouldn't they. I wished I had been one of them. Act one was entertaining enough but it had a big problem. It was followed by Act 2. The program notes say that here the show becomes more challenging and unpredictable. No. It becomes more obscure and incomprehensible, full of cleverdick wordplay and smartypants musical gymnastics with the phrasing and tempos. "Look at me! Look at me! Aren't I clever!" was the message. You may well be, but you are also boring. Definitely one for the Artistes. The Rest wisely stayed home, impervious to the arguments of the Straddlers.

I was to find out later that making a loss was factored into the discussion when the Committee decided to do it, on the grounds that "Joseph" will generate enough profit to cover the loss!

Sorry, my dear friends, but using the efforts of others in other shows to finance your artistic yearnings in a separate one is self-indulgence writ large. Losses happen but to deliberately incur one is irresponsible, and almost unforgiveable. It's hard enough to make a profit with any show but to budget for a loss is to court disaster because it eats into your reserves. Lady luck on her own, can bring you down easily enough. We nearly went bust once, just because of poor show selection, so there is no excuse to tempt fate deliberately.

So let's get back to a show that entertains the audience rather than baffles them.

I auditioned for Jacob and given I was the resident geriatric in the LTC, I had the inside running and got the part. Another jackpot! Minimal singing and no dancing, a couple of chances to overact and a photo in the program and the foyer. Once more, my cup runneth over.

The old adage that if you want full houses, put on a show with kids in it was never more evident. They really do bring an energy and joy to a production and after the heavy drama of the previous shows, it was welcome indeed.

We had a new Musical Director in Glenn Ross who we first saw as a member of Fagin's gang in "Oliver!" ten years previously. This was Christine Skicko's first outing as Director of our main Musical. Once upon a time we had serious trouble getting enough men to make up a chorus. Now they were available in abundance. There was enough for eleven brothers, several principals and some cameo roles and still have a couple left over. The Hicks's and the Diamentes were there in numbers.

Of course the first number to practice was the Dreamcoat song at the beginning and yours truly had to sing the opening line about Josephs' mother. There exists a DVD with me attempting this in the early stages of rehearsal .I could not have sung it worse if I had tried. I was as flat as the proverbial dunny man's hat. Pitching that opening note was to be the bane of my life right until performance and even then there was no certainty. What a dear, patient young man Glenn was. I then have the good fortune to exit the stage and off everyone else goes with the "red and blue and yellow and brown and green and orange and puce and liquorice and pistachio and tuttifrutti and cookies and cream and rum and raisin etc, etc, etc," with impressive choreography to match.

Jacob doesn't have too much else to do so I had the chance to watch it all unfold. It had been a long time since I saw everyone in a show having so much fun, adults and kids. One of the Principals was a bit up himself but eventually he woke up to himself. I wondered if the Director had had a wee word in his ear. Rehearsals were always good fun and as I didn't have much to do, was entertained every time and could see the progress made. Some of the kids started calling me grandpa! Cheeky little sods! The kids in the choir really blossomed. Glenn and Christine had a way with them that made them shine.

This year there was a change in the arrangements for the rehearsal camp in that there were a lot of kids involved and they could only be there in the daytime. The adults would arrive on the Friday night, work until about ten then socialise for while and then retire to be up bright-eyed and bushy-tailed for a full day and night of rehearsal, with the kids arriving after breakfast. Again it was a great opportunity to bring it all together as well as create a social bond amongst the cast and crew. The kids went home after the afternoon session. Costume fitting was also done as were make-up and hair styling workshops. By allowing my beard to grow to patriarchal splendour unhindered, I hardly needed to use much make up at all.

I have occasionally mentioned how we suffer for our art [mostly facetiously]. I will now present an example of this being the actual case. Two of the more well- muscled blokes were cast as attendants to the Pharaoh. In ancient Egypt they would have had their torsos and heads shaved. Our blokes did not need their heads shaved as they were wearing a nemes head covering, but they were to be bare-chested. So Andrew Hood and Keith Gibson-Williamson, saying that repeated shaving was inconvenient, volunteered to have their torsos waxed. I've always flinched when removing even a band-aid! Watching these two having the waxing done section by section over their whole upper body gave me the shivers. They had a huge audience who watched in gob-smacked amazement, especially the kids. The sight of those well-oiled pectorals and tight six-packs caused much oohing and aahing in the FC and, I might add, something similar in a certain section of the MC. True heroes in the cause of Art.

Sunday was a repeat until home time mid afternoon after we had cleaned up the place. Then it was Opening Night and another fabulous John Hall set.

I had not had so much fun in a show since "Pinafore/Trial" in 1982. I had little to do, so when I got chance to steal a scene, I seized it. In Act 2 there is the scene where all the brothers, having sold young Joe, have returned to Canaan, where everything has turned to shit because of drought. They sing that if they now invited someone to dinner, he might be on the menu [a la Hannibal Lector]. While this is going on I'm supposed to be sitting alone with Benjamin, nodding and gesticulating like a senile old git. Not me. When they sang the line about eating the guest, I did a double take that nearly ricked my neck. Got a laugh every time and the other blokes on the stage could not figure what was going on as I was well to the side of them, until some spoilsport let them in on the joke. Then they started looking in my direction instead of the audience. Michael Green [remember him?] strikes again.

Having so little to do, you would think that it would be difficult to cock anything up. Not at all. Because you're not involved for long stretches of time you lose your concentration. And so it happened. At the very end, when Joseph and his brothers have reconciled, old Jacob makes his entrance bearing the Technicolour Dreamcoat which Joseph duly puts on. How could you stuff that up? By getting nearly halfway across stage with fatherly arms outstretched and realising you have left said coat back in the wings. That's how! With some outlandish and exaggerated gestures to try to give the impression that this was all going to script, I had to make a rapid retreat into the wings and to then re-emerge with the bloody coat held aloft like Jason with the Golden Fleece. It only happened once but that was enough to incur admonishment. Then came the finale and encore. Of course the encore was to be all about "red and green" etc. which, as I was not in that song, I did not know. As well there were reprises of parts of various songs with appropriate dance moves, which also I did not know. So while everyone else was singing happily away and doing the right dance moves, I was just standing on the far left of the stage, just bopping along singing "it was red and red and red and red and red ". It was like in "Charlie Girl" with "fish and fish and fish", and it worked in this instance just as well.

Stand outs? The two characters who were on the stage for the whole show were Joseph and The Narrator and both Ben and Kara were excellent. The show consists of a number of ensemble pieces featuring various genres of music and all were done well, both in singing and choreography. Lawrie Fildes as the Pharoah/Elvis stole the show in his scenes. Of course the kids in the choir, singing their little hearts out, were a delight. At times I had flashbacks to my childhood, singing in the church and school choirs all those lifetimes ago.

It had been the most fun to have been in it. I think some of those "kids" are still with us in the LTC to this day.

The year closed on a happy note except that I still had a dental practice and no genuine buyers. Eager we were for 2007, as we were going to do "The Wizard of Oz". Choristers were to become Munchkins, Ozians and lots of other things.

There was to be only one show this year. From any point of view, this was going to be the biggest show we ever attempted and needed a full effort from the whole company. Even the ingenuity of John Hall and his team could not overcome the limitations of the Traralgon venue, so it was decided to use the Arts Centre at Warragul. To play in a real theatre was to be a treat. To play to a near full house in a 498 seat venue was to all but have a dream come true.

Before that happened, there was a lot of work to do and it was done with great enthusiasm. I had a lot more to do this time. I had scored the part of Uncle Henry/ Guard which involved quite a few scenes. This time my American accent had to be that. I took a while to get the drawl right but I did eventually. I also had to sing a couple of verses in "The Merry Old Land of Oz" at the start of Act 2 and learn a good bit of dialogue in other scenes.

As rehearsal gathered pace, I was continually fascinated by the Talent I was seeing. Unless something totally unexpected happened, this show was going to be a corker. And so it proved to be. We again had the rehearsal camp after which we could hardly wait to get into the theatre at Warrugal. It had been ten years since our last visit so not many of us had had the experience of performing in a REAL THEATRE! There were, however some problems that needed attention. There were probably heaps on the technical side of things but I was not privy to that. Getting entrances and exits right was problem enough for me as well as becoming acquainted with a certain little dog. I will 'fess up now that I do not like dogs at all and they soon sense it.

We had another John Hall masterpiece to perform on although I encountered two problems. The stage trapdoor had been built over to resemble a hurricane shelter. The actual hole was quite small so both Romy Eerhard, who played Aunt Em and was rather tall, and I, who was a bit tubby had difficulty getting down through it in the time allowed. As I was the last to get in I had to invent some mumblings to fill the time they took to climb down the hole into the back of the orchestra pit. It was then that I discovered a nailhead protruding from the edging of the wooden frame. Being still a practicing dentist, I was not too happy having an inch-long gouge taken out of the palm of my right hand. It was just as well that only recently I had had my tetanus booster. But it still bloodywell hurt for well over a week!

It also became evident that the peep door in the main gate of Oz was rather tiny, making it very difficult for me to poke my head through while wearing my big fur hat in order to bellow out my immortal line...."Who rang that bell?'. As the whole thing was made of steel, there was no chance of any alterations being made. Somehow I worked out a way to do it without losing my hat.

It is well known that theatres are dangerous places. We had been amazingly lucky over all these years that we had never had a serious injury to any of our company. That nearly came to a tragic end during the dress rehearsals when, one night, part of the Wicked Witches hut came loose and hit Max Maloney on the noggin, causing him to drop like a stone with concussion and bleeding freely. That finished rehearsal early in no uncertain fashion. Fortunately he was only slightly injured and was back on deck soon afterwards. By the time of the final dress rehearsal we were ready to shine.

Shine we did!

It would be extremely difficult to find a weak performance anywhere. It wasn't long before we knew we were in the presence of a star. Laura Hartnell was stunning as Dorothy. One of the great joys for me was to stand in the wings, listening to her sing "Over the Rainbow" night after night and each time bringing tears to my eyes and later when she is captive in the castle and cries out to Aunt Em how frightened she is, the same happened in the audience as well. Whenever I hear that song, I have Laura Hartnell in my mind more than Judy Garland. That's how good that kid was! To every scene she added a sparkle without even being aware of doing it.

Annette O'Shea as Miss Gulch and the Wicked Witch was right up there as well. A real nasty piece of work. The three male leads were also superb. You could be forgiven for thinking that those roles were written for THEM. A mention should be made of Wayne Musgrove who was the cowardly lion. This was only his second ever appearance in musical theatre. His first was as Simeon in "Joseph" the previous year. Talk about a hidden talent! Mark Woods was at his blustering best as the Professor/Wizard. But there was much more to this show than the Principals. There were Munchkins, Ozians, Blackbirds, Flowers, Flying Monkeys, Jitterbugs, Winkies, and more. Each and every one played their part in the success of the production. Costumes, especially costumes, make-up, hairstyling, pyrotechnics, light and sound, all had to be on a plane higher than anything we had done before. And, of course, they were.

The quality of the show meant that we had good houses and so made a sound profit, although we had to make a refund when Mother Nature decided to intervene.

It was a dark and stormy night and I had just finished my song about the "Merry Old Land of Oz" when there was a flickering of the lights and then all went dark. The power had been cut off by the storm. We had been advised during the pre-show fire drill that should this happen, you were stay where you were until directed to do otherwise by the Theatre Staff. We did exactly that. After some time had passed with the emergency lighting the only illumination, it was evident that it might be a while before power would be back, so the audience was offered a refund or a ticket for another night. Believe it or not, there were some people who complained to us about the interruption as if it was our fault.

For me this was the biggest production I had ever been in and the part I had the biggest yet. I enjoyed it immensely. Even the night I emerged from Oz to start singing my song about the Merry Old Land of Oz when a small voice pipes up from the audience..."It's Uncle Chris". Since you last met my niece Jacqui she had since married and had brought her darling daughter to the theatre. She was six. She got a bigger response from the audience than I did.

The show had been a mighty achievement for all concerned.

In retrospect, I would say, that for me, a third Golden Era had come to a close.

Our next show was to be a selection of a number of bits and pieces from our past shows called "Our Best Bits". I recalled such a show from 1979 which was a fizzer and "Toast to Broadway" also did not attract an audience. I really did not have much interest in being in it. I am told that it was well received and it made quite a tidy profit, so well done those who were in it. I had decided that since I had not had a holiday since 2002 it was time for one. The FDI Congress was to be in Dubai. I was going to attend as well as a couple of side trips to Scotland and to Jordan to see Petra. Petra was magical, everything it was cracked up to be. Glasgow a delightful revelation, far northern Scotland and the Orkneys, breathtaking, and Dubai a real dump.

At this time I was still the reluctant owner of a Dental Practice.

Our major show in 2008 was to be a revival of "Fiddler on the Roof". Although I knew it well, I was a bit apprehensive because I thought that no matter how good, I would not be able to avoid comparing it to the 1997 version.

When I arrived home I was informed that I had a serious buyer interested in the Practice. After two years was a sale in the offing?

# THE CURTAIN CLOSES.

The year 2008 was to be a major turning point in my life. At the end of 2007 I had a buyer for the practice and settlement was to be in mid February. I was to remain as an employee for four months to assist with the transition of Principals, with steadily reducing hours over that time. A great weight was to be lifted from my shoulders. It had been two years since it was put on the market and the more time passed without result in that period, the more downhearted I became. I was well aware that many country practices do not sell at all and, as with them, just closing the doors and walking away loomed as a decided possibility. Being able to perform with the LTC on stage was a major factor in me keeping my sanity. My gratitude is profound.

The New Year also brought some bad tidings. I received news that David Pickburn had been suddenly taken ill. Our relationship had been rather frosty since his departure in 2001. It soon became known that he had a brain tumour, the prognosis of which was equivocal. I think I heard it described as treatable but not curable. When that became known amongst those of us who remembered the parting of the ways, a very large penny dropped. We now had an explanation to David's uncharacteristic behaviour and attitude at the time. A mellowing of emotions would now start happening because we still held memories of the "old" David in our affections.

The season for Fiddler was to be in July at the West Gippsland Art Centre in Warragul so rehearsals started in February. I had the part of the Rabbi. My ability to grow a beard of patriarchal dimensions was to be handy one more time. The need for authenticity that had permeated our previous production of "Fiddler" was also needed for this one as well so I went to Melbourne's Jewish Museum in St Kilda to get advice as to how I should portray the Rabbi. They were most helpful about how to hold your hands whilst praying and other gestures and gave me a list of things I needed such as prayer shawls that could be purchased at Gold's Emporium in Balaclava in Melbourne. I was even able to purchase a black yamulke with the emblem of the Melbourne Football Club on it. I even wore it in the show a couple of times until Christine, the Director, spotted it. Admonishment right until the end! I even I was able to purchase a book of blessings in Hebrew which I was going to include in the scene where Motel unveils his new sewing machine.

It was great to be back rehearsing such an iconic show as "Fiddler" but it did not have the same thrill as doing it the first time and I felt it didn't have that feeling of "Jewishness" that had so characterised the 1997 production. That understanding and feeling of empathy with both the people and their faith is crucial if you are to give a convincing performance. In '97 the Directors pushed us to BE our characters, not just play them. Unfortunately, this did not seem to be the case this time. No such direction was forthcoming. When it came to the rehearsal camp I brought a book I had obtained about the life in the shtetles of middle Europe for anyone to have a look at and get an idea of what a real Anatevka looked like. Not one person took up the offer. Maybe I was just getting a little fixated on that aspect of it but that degree of diffidence was disappointing. On another occasion I asked the directing team about me, being the Rabbi, having a cylinder made to represent the container made for transporting the Torah scrolls. I had a good friend who was willing to make the appropriate decorated cloth cover for it. The idea met with blank looks and then a dismissive approval for me to make one myself. I had neither the tools nor the expertise to do it. In times past, someone like Dave Sargeson would have knocked it up in a couple of hours. No such assistance was forthcoming. The significance of the request was lost on the directing team. When everyone was leaving the village, the Rabbi's family would be carrying all their material belongings. The Rabbi would be carrying the Torah scrolls from the synagogue, which to him would be worth far more than all his earthly possessions. Blank looks were accompanied by deaf ears.

On the plus side, I had become a new man after achieving a sale of the practice. It was an odd feeling, working for wages again after all these years of being my own boss. On one Friday in mid February I owned a dental practice. On the next Monday I didn't. When I finished work on that Monday, I looked across the hallway of the building to the office and thought to myself, "That's not my office anymore. I don't have to go in there any more to do another hours' paperwork". And I never did, right up to my final day there, which was to be a week after the end of the season of Fiddler. A mighty weight had been lifted from my shoulders. I'm sure I walked taller and with straighter shoulders from that Monday on. Even though it was a Monday, I went straight down to the Morwell Club and had a celebratory drink. A large one.

Rehearsals did not seem to go smoothly. There always seemed be changes being made right up until the season opened. The circular choreography of the opening number was still being worked out when we moved into the theatre. Those of us who had been in the 97 version, pointed out on numerous occasions during the rehearsal period, that a crucial part of the chorus singing needed to be addressed as it had not been practiced at all during that time. It appeared to me that the directing team finally took notice of this only when we were in the theatre! The piece in question occurs when Tevye disowns his daughter Chava when she tells him she wishes to marry outside the faith. As he leaves her she cries"Papa, Papa" at which the Chorus sings "Tradition " three times in ascending pitch from off-stage. How that was to be done and how to see the conductor was worked out from scratch in the theatre in the final rehearsals. Needless to say, it was ragged.

For those who had never been in Fiddler before, it was a great experience. For those who had been in the 97 version, it was a bit of a letdown. That is not to say there weren't some great performances. It was a good show. In the memory, it had to compete with a truly great show. Denise Twite as Fruma Sara was scary. Dale Gemmell was a good Perchik but Samantha Grumley as Chava was the pick. Her Chava was a heartfelt performance. As for me, my big moment comes at the end of Act 1 when I dance at the wedding to the disgust of my prig of a son, Mendel. All was going to plan until one night my boots slipped on the floor and I landed square on my arse to the gasp of the chorus who knew this was not intentional, and the laughter of the audience who thought it was. I was helped to my feet as the scene progressed with my usual exaggerated gestures as if nothing untoward had happened. At interval, anyone who suggested I do it each performance was given short shrift. I had a sore quoit for several weeks. I made damn sure I didn't do that again. I was getting too old for that to happen more than once.

I mentioned earlier how I managed to insert a real prayer into the sewing machine scene. It just felt appropriate and my thanks to the people at Gold's Emporium. In our alphabet it goes something like this: "Boruch atoh adonoy, elohaynu melech ho-olom." {You are blessed, Lord our God, the Sovereign of the world"}. It is a general blessing for the enjoyment of various benefits. Best ad-lib I ever did.

It was during the season that I had an experience that has perplexed me ever since. It was after one of the matinee shows. I was getting changed when one of our FOH people came down to the dressing room to tell me that an old friend was in the foyer and wanted to say hello. In due course out I went. Well; If you had asked me beforehand to have a thousand guesses as who it was I would not have succeeded. I had not seen Joanne Hill since I worked at the Rosstown Hotel when I was at university about 35 years ago. At that time she was Joanne Johnson. With her was her son whose name I now forget. They had seen my name in the program. Our fathers had been great friends from the days they worked at the Trotting Control Board of Victoria.{Now known as Harness Racing Victoria} in the 1950's and 60's. Her father Len had left the TCB to manage the Rosstown Hotel. In those days it was one of the biggest and busiest pubs in Melbourne. We Billings boys had known the Johnson girls all our lives. I had even taken Joanne to the Matriculation School Dance at De La Salle College in 1966 at the tender age of 16. She would have been no older than 15. Nothing serious came of it. We were just kids. Well, I was. She subsequently married a chap called Bill who had a property at Labertouche, not far from Warragul. We had a good old chinwag and agreed to keep in touch. We exchanged Xmas greetings and arranged to meet after I had finished my locum in Mansfield in Feb 2009. It was not to be. Everyone in Victoria is aware that in Feb 2009 the Black Saturday fires erupted with catastrophic results. In the two weeks prior to that, there were fires in Gippsland in the hills near Boolarra and in the area around Labertouche. Their property was ravaged and their house was only saved in the nick of time by a water-bombing helicopter. Bill was badly burned and would have perished but for the bravery of their son. His face was on the front page of the Herald-Sun. He survived. When I returned to Morwell to renew contact, I was greeted with the news that Joanne had died suddenly from a heart attack. The workings of Fate are strange. You meet up with someone you haven't seen for decades, make plans to renew the friendship and then: gone.

I could go on about what I felt was lacking in the show but there is no point. It went well enough and some lessons were learned. Everyone who was in it, came away enriched. It was just a matter of how much. At this time I was informed that treatment had been successful in stabilising David Pickburn's condition so I thought I could wait to see him after my trip overseas.

After this show I was going to have the holiday for which I had worked for 33 years to enjoy. I was taking a round the world trip, flying business class. The FDI Congress was in Stockholm. I was going to attend that after I had visited St. Petersburg's Hermitage museum and then spending time in the Baltic States, Estonia, Latvia, and Lithuania.

St. Petersburg was a stunner. The Hermitage Museum was even more so. To stand in a room that has a Leonardo at one end, a Michelangelo at the other, with a Raphael in the middle is quite an eye-opener. Then on to the Impressionists. You name the artist; there is at least one of his in the collection, quite possibly a room full. Then you go to the Summer Palace to see the Amber Room. Quite amazing what you can build or buy when money is no object. I had intended to limit my time in Russia to the days I spent in St. Petersburg. The Russian Immigration Police had other ideas. I was on the overnight sleeper to Tallinn, when at 2.00 am on reaching the border, I was informed that my visa had expired at midnight so I would have to leave the train and report to the Immigration Police office at 9.00 to obtain a new visa. The whole farce that followed is quite a story in itself [2], but I was the guest of the Russians Police for 12 hours in the splendid metropolis on Ivangorod. If Russia has an arsehole, then Ivangorod is the haemorrhoid upon it.

The difference between a free country like Estonia and Russia is palpable. Tallinn was the highlight of the whole trip. Beautiful, historical, welcoming city it is. It was fortunate that the War more or less bypassed it. The three Baltic states had been part of the Russian Empire for a couple of centuries before WW1 but with the collapse of Tsarist Russia they became independent states, as did Poland. With the pact between Stalin and Hitler made, the Russians very quickly moved back in with a vengeance. Tallinn has a Museum of the Deportations. Estonia did not have a large Jewish presence so the Holocaust did not affect its general population all that much. To Stalin and the NKVD being Estonian was enough.

Riga, the capital of Latvia has an excellent holocaust Museum. Grim and truthful. The Jewish holocaust was far more extensive here, but it was even more so in Lithuania. In its Capital, Vilnius, there are two museums worth visiting. First is the KGB building which just as it was in 1991 when the KGB moved out. Terrible things happened there. The other is a rather small Jewish museum of the Holocaust. There is virtually no trace of the Jewish presence in the city that was once called "the Jerusalem of the North". When I visited I was told that even in 2008 they are abused and vandalised. After visiting

---

2 Although it has nothing to do with the LTC, I have included the story as an appendix. As I said at the very beginning: I am not making this up!

these countries and learning something of their histories, it is no wonder they dislike and fear the Russians. Touring the lands where "Fiddler" was set after just finishing the season was another emotional experience. I even started to picture doing a follow-up "investigation" as to the ultimate fate of the characters in "Fiddler"

After having attended the Congress in Sweden [a country that can cause serious damage to the wallet], I was pondering how I was going to be able to be in "Beauty and the Beast" which was to be our major show in 2009. I had already secured my first locum position when I returned home in October. I told myself the picture might be a bit clearer after I did my first locum. That was to be in Ballarat and it was to start just ten days after I got home. Those ten days were extremely busy so I postponed visiting David as I was under the impression that he was faring all right.

To Ballarat I went. My first experience as a locum went very well and Dr.Virginia Williams and her husband Hugh are friends to this day. Whilst in Ballarat my second job was forthcoming and it was to be in Mansfield in January. As time passed, offers of jobs started coming in from all over the country and it became apparent that, as I would be spending a lot of time away interstate, I would not be at home long enough to do the necessary rehearsals. It dawned on me that I had probably been in my last show. No point auditioning if you can't make rehearsals.

I finished in Ballarat just over a week before Xmas. It was my turn to host the Billings Family Xmas which meant catering for about 30 people, young and old. It was a busy week. It was during this week I heard that David had taken a serious turn for the worst. I thought I had time to see him after my family day, but such was not to be the case. He passed away that week. To this day, I have bitterly rued the decision to delay going to see him until I got home from Ballarat. I thought I had time. I didn't.

David's funeral was at the West Gippsland Arts Centre. It was a full house. He was centre stage. Tributes were many and heartfelt. Just prior to his funeral someone showed me a sequence on their phone showing David resting by the window of his house not long before he died. What I saw there was the essence of the David we all had known and loved before his illness stole the real David from us. I saw a man who was physically wasted by his illness but his love for life and the knowledge of a life well lived still shone through by way of a tiny wan smile. Ecce Homo.

I'm sure Heaven had room for a Modern Major-General. Vale David Pickburn.

After the funeral I drove down to Melbourne to meet up with my brother and we would then head north for our annual road trip {aka the booze cruise}. I had to stop a couple of times on the way as I had trouble seeing the road. It was a bright summer's day. I couldn't see for the tears. Even now, after twelve years, the same is happening as I write these lines.

With that the curtain has closed.

# POSTSCRIPT

It turned out that "Fiddler on the Roof" was my last hurrah on the stage. My new role as a locum dentist required me to travel all over the country for varying periods of time and I never quite knew where I would be going next so there was no way I could commit to being available for either rehearsal or for the performance of the actual show. I did retain my commitment to the position of Public Officer until changes to the relevant legislation placed the Public Officer's duties with the secretary. I was pleased I was asked to do it and it had kept me in touch a bit.

I tried to attend as many of the shows as I could but it was not possible to attend all of them, so that is the main reason I finished my memoir at 2008, as well as not being able to be actually involved in the shows themselves. Someone else can take up a pen [keyboard] to fill the years after 2008. By selling the practice I was able to shed the source of a lot of stress in my life and was able to practice my profession for another 12 years until the end of 2019 when I turned 70 and thought, "that's enough". As a student and graduate, I had been in the game for 52 years. The last 12 years had been a good gig. I was paid to work in interesting places with my travel and accommodation paid for and most times the use of a motor vehicle as well.

I did have one interesting experience relating to my time in the LTC. I was back in Ballarat in November 2009. I was passing a pub one Saturday afternoon when I heard a voice cry out "Doc!" I turned around and there was Jaz Flowers in the doorway! She had just graduated from the Victorian School of the Arts and was celebrating. She invited me to join her and she graciously introduced me to her friends who welcomed me cheerfully. I was a little embarrassed at first. Here was I, the old squeeze-your-cheeks-together tenor discussing musical theatre with all these very talented youngsters whose future could be anything. We all had a very pleasant hour or so. To prove my point, I next met Jaz at the stage door of the Princess Theatre after seeing her as the lead in the Melbourne production of "Hair Spray". She was still the same friendly, unaffected girl we knew from her time in the LTC.

Another event that should be noted was the passing of Jean Dougan in March 2011. I was at home at that time so was able to attend the funeral which was attended by a good roll-up of LLOS/LTC members. We were there to say farewell to our adopted granny whom we all loved.

During the time I was actively involved with the LLOS/LTC I saw quite a lot of very talented people on that stage, and lot behind and in front of it as well. So I suppose I should let you know what I thought to be the best.

My number one show was "Fiddler on the Roof",1997 version. After that there are a number of shows that I regard very highly.

West side Story, Cabaret, Hello Dolly, Wizard of Oz, My Fair Lady, Annie, HMS Pinafore/Trial by Jury, Iolanthe, Pirates of Penzance 1993 version and Noises Off.

I had the pleasure and privilege of seeing and hearing some wonderful performances, in particular seeing four young lasses make their debuts as Principals. I shall introduce them in chronological order:

- Joy Sim as Josephine in HMS Pinafore 1982
- Emmy Coleman as Eliza in My Fair Lady 1998
- Jessie Waugh as Maria in West Side Story 2004
- Laura Hartnell as Dorothy in Wizard of Oz 2007
- Everyone of those was a standout performance.

Other great female performances in no particular order:

- Kara Smith as Sally Bowles in Cabaret 2005
- Betty Clark as The Countess of Plazatoro in The Gondoliers 1980
- Pam Hoppe as Golde in Fiddle on the Roof 1997

- Christine Skicko as Dolly in Hello Dolly 2003
- Wendy Bradley as Charlie in Charlie Girl 1994

Of course there were some very memorable performances from the men as well.

- Top of the list is Bryce Sedgwick as the MC in Cabaret 2005]. I regard his as the best performance of a principal, male or female, I ever saw in my time in the company. It was a toss-up between him and Laura Hartnell in Wizard of Oz for that accolade.

My other top performances were:

- John Black as Tevye in Fiddler on the Roof 1997
- Nick Kong as Tony in West Side Story 2005
- Lawrie Fildes as Fagin in Oliver! 1996 and as Warbucks in Annie 2000 and Alfred Doolittle in My Fair Lady 1998
- David Pickburn in all the G&S Canon
- George Murphy as the Grand Inquisitor in The Gondoliers 1980
- Ernie Rijs as Dick Deadeye in HMS Pinafore 1982 and Grosvenor in Patience 1984
- Simon Hemming, Wayne Musgrove and Anthony Di Donato as the Tin Man, the Cowardly Lion and the Scarecrow respectively in Wizard of Oz. 2007

Since 2008 I have seen some really good stuff, but I have missed a lot as well. Here's a few that I reckon were pretty good:

- Hairspray. Best thing I saw Bernard Dettering do. Similarly for Daniel Hanson. Great performance from Georgia Moore. Quite a step from being a kid in the choir in Joseph.
- Sound of Music. Knock out Finale from Mary Mirtschin. Her voice did not need a mic. Brodie Dorling was also great as Maria.
- Footloose. Some great ensemble work, especially the dance sequence.
- The Little Mermaid. Another top performance by Bernard Dettering as King Triton. Christina Poihipi as Sebastian and Scott Millar as Scuttle were excellent. However the stand out

with this show was the make-up, costumes and the lighting. Spectacular!

- Sweet Charity. Kara Smith in excellent form once again. However, to me the performance of Craigen Whitehead was the standout. It was the best thing he has done in all the years he has been with the company. You could easily think that the part of Oscar Lindquist was written for him.

Of course all of the above is just my opinion. After all, I was never an Artiste. I was just one of the Rest. And enjoyed every minute of it.

Of course there was always great chorus and ensemble work and wonderful and imaginative sets on which we could all strut our stuff.

The last thing to do is to thank all those hundreds of people I met who made this experience possible. I knew many of you all too fleetingly, and sadly, I have forgotten a lot of your names but you were all a part of it. Many of you I have now known for many years and forged firm friendships, and when we meet the memories quickly emerge along with the laughter. There were trying times on occasion but overall I have loved every minute of my involvement with you all and I hope I have not been too big a pain in the neck to you. I have used everyone's real names as I think, should this memoir ever be published, all of you deserve to be acknowledged for your part in making the LTC the wonderful company it is. You all deserve to be more than just a name in the program. In the words of the great Jeff Fenech," I love youse all!"

The idea of writing this memoir arose from conversations had with a number of old faces after the funeral of the wonderful Barbara Derham. "One day I'll get around to that" I said to myself. That day arrived not long after a little thing called Covid 19 arrived from China and we went into lockdown. There was bugger-all else to do so I took to the keyboard and here we are. In putting all this to paper, I have been helped by my dear friend and fellow committee member, and Life Member Kate Dougan who was able to help me get my dates and years right and also have long discussions about times past, although she is still very much in the present with the Company.

At the moment there is no live theatre and people are more and more being forced to live via the internet, with actual face to face contact being actively discouraged or even being made illegal. Pessimists amongst us even fear that live theatre will wither away. I beg to differ.

Right from pre-history Man has participated in theatre. When Man first stencilled the outline of his hand or painted familiar animals onto the walls of Lascaux, Altamira or Arnhem Land, painted his body and danced in the firelight beneath them, accompanied by chanting and the clapping of special sticks together, he was indulging in a musical theatrical performance.

The ancient Greeks gave it the modern form we know in Western culture. But musical theatre exists in many forms around the world. There in an innate need for man and woman to perform with the tribe, the family, the village or the language group because Man is a social being who needs to be part of the group. When this pandemic passes, as it surely will do, I reckon live theatre will be back with a vengeance and I just hope to be around to see the LTC in the forefront of that resurgence.

It might just coincide with the completion of the Latrobe City Performing Arts Centre. You never know your luck in a big city.

**Chris Billings**

## LEAVING MOTHER RUSSIA

**A day in the life of Christoff Michaelavitch**

My plan had been to take the overnight sleeper train from St.Petersburg to Tallinn. It left St.Petersburg at 11.00pm and arrived in Tallinn at 6.00am next morning. My visa was valid until the day of my departure. If I had been flying then there would have been no problem as emigration is done at the airport. However, that is not the case with rail travel in Russia. The paper work is done at the border, although it could have been done at the departing station as the train is a non-stop express whilst in Russia. When the train reached the border at about 2.00am my visa had expired at midnight. I was informed rather brusquely by one of the immigration officials that I must leave the train. I wasn't going to argue, so gathering up my bags, off the train I went. It isn't very warm in those parts at 2.00am. I was taken to a rather smart new office building at the station where I was met by a young officer who spoke impeccable English and was quite polite. I was then interviewed by him for a good half hour on a wide range of subjects but often coming back to whether or not I had been in the military and more specifically had I been in Vietnam during the war. Although I was pissed off and tired I made sure I was as polite and straightforward as could be. No smart arse comments or jokes. Having determined that I didn't have a licence to kill, he offered me the choice of staying in the waiting room of the police building or going into town to stay at the hotel. Irrespective of my choice I had to report to the local police at 9.00am. As the station was warm and the toilets and wash room were available, and it was 3.00am, I opted to stay where I was. He informed me that a taxi would arrive for me at 9.00am.

I then faced the task of trying to get some sleep. The only items of "furniture" available were two metal benches, fixed to the floor and divided into four by fixed armrests. There was no way to stretch out. I soon came to the conclusion that these benches were really just subtle instruments of torture. After some fitful sleep, daylight came and so did the morning shift of police who walked around the building as if I wasn't there. At 9.00am the taxi arrived. I've seen some clapped out shitboxes of cars in my time {even driven some in my student days} but this old mid- eighties Nissan was up there with them. Still, it beat walking. On the payment of two hundred roubles, off we went to the local police station.

It soon became obvious that the suspension of the taxi was all but non-existent. The roads on this earthly paradise of Ivangorod consisted of potholes of varying and sometimes frightening dimensions, interlaced with ribbons of tarmac. Every time the taxi hit one of these bomb craters your backside knew about it first and then the rest of your spine. In due course we arrived at the Police Station and what a sight it was.

The state of this building made the Nissan look like it had just come off the assembly line. I don't know which Tsar commissioned it, but it would have to have been a couple before the last one and I don't think it had seen a paint brush since. As I got out of the taxi, I was met by a police woman who ushered me into the building, pointed to a room where I could leave my bags, and then into what I took to be an interview room. Apparently they were expecting me. The inside of the building was dark and gloomy and little better than the outside, with only about half the light globes working, and these must have been the last remaining ten watt globes on earth. Luckily it was a sunny day and there was no point having curtains on the windows as the dirt on them rendered them quite opaque. The light globes working or not, were all liberally sprinkled with fly poo. To top it off, the whole place stank like a public dunny. I started to feel sorry for the poor bastards that had to work here, but I soon got over it.

I was not the only person in that interview room. There were two others. One was a young woman and the other was an older man. The latter was to become a significant part of this story. After a while, another policewoman arrived and gave us all what I assumed was a ticking off for our evil designs on Mother Russia. She then produced some forms to be filled out and left us to it. Now, government forms, no matter which country they are from are often a challenge to get right. It is doubly difficult when they have been "translated" into English and the original is written in the Cyrillic alphabet. The other two people managed to do it rather easily but not me. It was now that the older man who sat next to me offered to help. I readily accepted his help although he spoke only a bit of English and I spoke no Russian at all. We introduced ourselves. His name was Pavel and he came from Estonia. When I said I came from Australia the look he gave me showed that I must have been the first he had ever met. He smiled and said "kangaroo". I thought "this blokes all right". With his help, I filled out the forms and waited for the policewoman to return which she did after some time, during which Pavel and I managed to converse with one another. When the copper returned she spoke to the woman who was with us and then ushered her out of the room. A couple minutes later the copper reappeared and spoke to us. It appeared that we were both in the same boat regarding our visas. I got the impression that this was not the first time Pavel had been in this situation. He knew what we had to do and said I should come with him. As I had no better offer, I did. In the back of my mind I still had visions of the KGB and the Gulag. Anyway, out of the station we emerged. We were a couple of kilometres from the centre of the town so we got into the taxi that was waiting outside the police station. This one had a functioning suspension that made falling into the bomb craters marginally less bone rattling. What it did not have was a functioning clutch. Every gear change had you jerking back and forth. We were heading for our first stop which was the bank. When we got there it was another 200 roubles, EACH, thank you. I thought "Every bugger in town is in on this racket"! Pavel sorted him out in no uncertain manner. It was 200 roubles for both of us.

We went into the bank which was a reasonably new building. That was two I had seen now. We presented our forms and were growled at in Russian to follow the teller outside to the ATM, the existence of which mildly surprised me. We each extracted 800 roubles and clutching our treasure went back inside the bank where we were relieved of our roubles with much stamping of forms and dire warnings not to lose the forms or the receipts. Our next stop was to get new photos for our new visas. The photographers' shop was not far away so we walked.

I don't think in all my travels I have seen a sorrier place. I have already described the roads. The central park had been denuded of any flower beds or lawns. What wasn't bare earth was covered with weeds. The concrete of the footpaths was cracked and uneven, the guttering broken. There was an open air market place where about half a dozen old babushkas were offering produce for sale. Some withered carrots, some spuds but not much else. There was one old bloke with a stall offering clothing that looked like it came from a Vinnies' store thirty years ago. If ever Ivangorod was looking for a twin city arrangement in another country, I reckon Pompeii would be a good match.

We reached the photographer's shop and entered. There was no one there so Pavel gave the bell a good ring. We could hear someone coming from the room behind the shop. A curtain was pushed aside and into the shop sashayed the photographer. I had to turn my back as I could barely stop myself from bursting out laughing.

Anyone familiar with the comedy "Little Britain" will know of " Dafydd,the only gay in the village". Well, his Russian counterpart stood before us. At the risk of invoking stereotypes, he could have just as easily stepped off the set of the Benny Hill Show. His hair was curled into a perm. He was wearing a Paisley body shirt and flared trousers. I could not see if he was wearing platform shoes. And the wrist was limp. Pavel gave me a kick in the ankle as I turned back again to take in the vision, still struggling to stop laughing. I near bit my tongue in half. Pavel explained what we needed and we proceeded to have our photos taken. I shall call our friend Ivan. Ivan then produced a camera that resembled one of those old Polariods that processed the film immediately but was not so advanced. He took special care to position us and then took the shots and advised us that we should come back in an hour. I was still smirking as we left and even dour old Pavel had a smile on his face. What to do for the next hour? Pavel came to the rescue. He invited me to join him back at the hotel for some lunch. Given that I had had nothing to eat since dinner the previous evening, I did not need a second invitation, so to the hotel we went. But not without a deviation to the "supermarket". This was the third and last modern building in Ivangorod that I saw. This building had the surface area of about two double garages. About 20% of the space was given over for groceries and 80% to alcohol. Pavel was interested in the latter, from which he bought a bottle of what turned out to be a rather delicious Estonian fruit wine, about the strength of port. With that we headed for the hotel.

This was the hotel that was offered to me when I was taken off the train. I' m glad I declined.

The hotel was four- storied and built in that exquisitely ugly style that Eastern Bloc architects had given the world in the 1960s and 70s. It has seen better days, a situation that probably started to occur the day after it was completed. It was what the Russians thought that a stylish modern hotel should be from watching too many films from Hollywood. Judging by the number of things not working, it had also been built with their usual attention to detail and pride in their craftsmanship. In the foyer there was a hairdressers' which was open and peopled by three ladies of a certain vintage who were all bottle blonde with beehive hairstyles and all looked remarkably like Jane Turner as the Russian newsreader in "FastForward". There was also a Gift Shop where one could purchase papers and magazines, cigarettes, postcards, souvenirs and all the various knickknacks that the sophisticated traveller of the 1970's could need. Apart from the newspapers and cigarettes everything else had a layer of dust on it. There were no customers. A souvenir of bloody Ivangorod was about the last thing on earth I wanted. There was a Coffee Shop but it was closed, as was the dining room. My vision of a sitting down to a nice lunch evaporated. Pavel indicated I should follow him up to his room. I had little choice but to do what he said but some dark and uncomfortable thoughts were entering my head. What was this bloke up to?

His room was on the second floor so up the stairs we went as the lift was out of order. It was no great deal as I was still quite spritely in those days.

His room could perhaps be described as Spartan. It was clean enough but not very big. The furniture was a Russian version of IKEA and I'm sure the shower cubicle once had its walls completely covered with tiles. There was a table with two chairs, one of which I sat on rather carefully. Pavel then produced the bottle of plonk and two glasses into which he poured some of its contents. As we drank to each other's health, he opened a suitcase that was lying on the bed to take out the contents. I could not have more surprised if he had produced a giant live rabbit. What he did produce was the jacket and cap from the dress uniform of a full colonel of the Soviet Red Army, complete with an array of medals and other decorations. Well, this day was turning out to be one like no other! He then proceeded to put them on. Pavel was of average height but when he put the jacket and cap on and straightened his back, the change was incredible. He now looked quite formidable. He then took the uniform off and carefully packed it away. He next opened his other case, from which he took a plastic supermarket bag which contained some bread, tomatoes, cheese, sausage and dill pickles which he spread out on the table for us to share, along with the plonk. I was that hungry I could have bitten the bum out of a rag doll. I now began to feel ashamed of the uncharitable thoughts I had entertained not that long ago. While we were eating, I managed to learn his story.

He was Estonian and had been a colonel in the Soviet Army. When the USSR collapsed he was near retirement. On his retirement, he elected to live in Estonia which by then was an independent country.

To show their gratitude, the Russians said that since he was now a citizen of another country, they should pay him his pension. The Estonians disagreed. Eventually the Russians conceded but all too often his payments are not paid. So every so often he goes to St.Petersburg to argue his case in full uniform just to remind them of his service to them. On the way back to Estonia they occasionally take him off the train and put him through the shakedown that I was now experiencing. I had suspected that he had been through this nonsense before. I could not help thinking that when it comes to being arseholes, the Russian bureaucracy sets the Gold Standard. This bloke wasn't up to anything except being a decent, kind human being who wanted someone to hear his story. He never mentioned any family so assumed that he had none. A look at his watch prompted him to finish packing his bags and for us to head off to the photographer. We made sure we finished the plonk before we left. I was honoured to carry one of his cases. Some food and half a bottle of fortified wine had made my mood lighten markedly.

After another short walk in the sunshine, we arrived at Ivan's. He must have heard us coming, because as we entered he flounced into the shop and greeted us with a bonhomie that suggested we had known each other for years, and with a flourish presented us with our photos after the payment of four hundred roubles, each. Everyone with a passport knows that the idea behind the photos is to make the person on them look as sinister as possible. Ivan had achieved this in full measure. Being in black and white probably helped. Our less than delighted reaction to seeing our photos left Ivan rather crestfallen as we left. But we had all we needed for the coppers, so back to the station we went. Another clapped out taxi, another 200 roubles.

On arrival at the police station, we presented our documents to the copper at the entrance and were directed to the room we had occupied earlier in the day and told to wait. It was getting into the afternoon and I was wondering if I was destined to spend another night on the banks of the Narva river. If so, I was hoping to God it would be on the Estonian side. But no! Just as these thoughts were entering my head, our “friendly” police woman appeared with our passports and new visas and other paperwork needed to leave the workers’ paradise of Russia. The new visa was printed on a piece of paper the size of a single piece of toilet paper and just about as robust. All bloody day to produce this! After giving us these documents she basically said, in their usual friendly manner, pick up your luggage from the storeroom and piss off and don’t do it again. I had no intention of doing it again but I had the feeling that Pavel may, whether he wanted to or not. As we left the police station, there was the ubiquitous taxi waiting outside. This one actually had everything working and a driver who spoke some English. Where had you been all day? To the border crossing asp in case they change their minds. Another 200 roubles. Couldn’t pay it quick enough.

On entering the building we were directed to different exit lines. As I approached the counter I saw the Immigration Officer was a stunning dark-haired young woman in an immaculately tailored uniform. If the sight of a beautiful woman in uniforms tickles your ivories then you would have loved to have been there. In contrast, I would have looked like some old hobo who had been dragged through a hedge backwards and ponged like one of the critters that lived in that hedge. Nevertheless, she gave me a winning smile as I handed over my documents. On perusing them she looked at me and said, ”Excuse me just a minute,” in impeccable English and disappeared into an office just behind her stool. When that happened, I dropped my shoulders, looked to the heavens and uttered rather too loudly,” What the f**k’s wrong now?” After a minute or two, she re-appeared and, all smiles, stamped every piece of paper in her possession, handed them to me and, as she waved me through, bid me “Have nice day”. “HAVE A NICE DAY!!! HAVE A F**CKING NICE DAY!!!!! “ Most of its gone thanks to you mob of bastards and I’m still in bloody Narva!

But I speedily made my way across the bridge to seek the sanctuary of Estonia. As I did so I could see that there was something to see in Ivangorod. There are two magnificent fortresses from the late medieval period on either side of the Narva River. One was built by

Ivan IV known as the Terrible and after whom the town was named. The other was built by Germanic Knights of the Order of the Sword who ruled Estonia at that time when Tallinn was known as Reval and was a city of the Hanseatic League. Must come back and see them one day I thought. Fat chance of that ever happening. I sailed through the Estonian border. As I emerged from the Estonian border post, I looked back across the river. Much to the amusement of the Estonians, I then proceeded to tell those on the other side what I thought of them and their town, rather loudly. In the two or three minutes it took to do this I don't think I used the same word twice. I was almost tempted to give them a "moon". I decided not to as I didn't fancy a Kalashnikov bullet fired by a cranky Russia border guard up my cloaca .Meanwhile, Pavel who had sailed through the border without any hassles, had found the next express bus to Tallinn and had even bought the tickets. He was probably on first name terms with the border officials by now.

The contrast between Narva and Ivangorod could not have been more stark. Ivangorod I described earlier. Narva was the complete opposite. It had modern shops, all of which were stocked with goods. It had cafes and bars. Its streets had no potholes. The footpaths were even and devoid of weeds. The park had lush grass and flower beds. It had hotels that were built this century. Mostly, it had people who smiled.

It only took a couple of hours to get to Tallinn but I could not keep awake. I was roused as the bus arrived on the outskirts of Tallinn. After we disembarked at the bus station, I insisted to Pavel to allow me to buy him a coffee, which he graciously did. At this point we both knew that there was nothing else to say, so we went our separate ways. In the cab to the hotel, I pondered on the fact that I had just met a wonderful human being and I hoped upon hope that the Russians would treat him as such. But I doubt it.

When I got to the hotel, it was nearly 6.00pm. After checking in, I had a lovely hot shower, put on some fresh clothes and had a couple of beers, a good feed, and then the sleep of the just.

Everything in this story is true!

## Be Published